# Puppets, Kids, and Christian Education

by Kurt Hunter

Firelight

**Augsburg Fortress**

# Contents

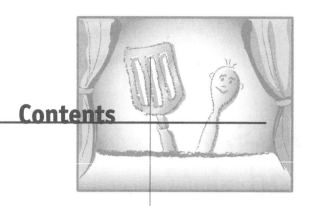

PUPPETS, KIDS,
AND CHRISTIAN EDUCATION
by Kurt Hunter

Editors: Kristen Glass
and Carolyn Berge
Cover: Marti Naughton
Interior design: Mike Mihelich
Photos: © 2001 PhotoDisc (background,
top); Eyewire (middle, bottom)
Diagrams, patterns, and interior photos:
Kurt Hunter

ISBN 0-8066-6409-6

Manufactured in the U.S.A.

05 04 03 02 01 1 2 3 4 5 6 7 8 9 10

# Puppetry and Bible Learning

Amazing things have been happening in our Sunday school program for the last several years. Our kids are excited to come to church and they don't want to leave when it's over, and they're even bringing friends with them. Leaders are having fun too. Best of all, the kids are getting directly involved with the stories of the Bible and understanding and remembering them like never before.

The "transformation" began in the spring of 1996, when Ardys Sabin, the director of Christian education at my church, Spirit of Hope United Methodist, in Golden Valley, Minnesota, spearheaded a move to transform our Sunday school program. We moved from a traditional classroom model to the lab-based, hands-on, rotation-style model. That transformation was the most exciting thing that I have ever experienced in the church.

People learn in different ways, so the material being taught should be reinforced in different ways. For several weeks, a Sunday school will cover the same material and the students will rotate each week to a different workshop or lab.

We transformed our existing classrooms into seven labs: "Thou Art," an arts and crafts studio; "The Church Mouse," a computer lab; "Father Abraham's Arcade," a game room; "Abundant Life Theater," a video theater; "Matter of Faith," a science center, "Mary and Martha's Kitchen," and "Parable Productions," a drama and puppetry room. As the church's resident puppeteer, I was asked to put the puppetry program in place.

My own fascination with puppetry began in the mid 1970s, when I saw an incredible marionette show at an arts festival during a family vacation to California. When we got home, I got books from the local library and began making my own marionettes. I soon joined the Puppeteers of America and learned more about the world of puppetry. Since then, I've had opportunities to perform with professional puppet companies and also as a solo puppeteer. I've worked with puppets of every shape and size in many different settings including television and orchestra concerts. Over the years, I've also seen a great deal of the best puppetry that the world has to offer and have had opportunities to learn firsthand from some of the world's finest puppeteers.

It was from this broad base in puppetry that I dove into the creation of our puppetry lab. I think it had always bothered me that Sunday school was something that kids tended to tolerate rather than be interested in or excited about. Our move to rotation-style learning changed that completely. Suddenly, Sunday school was something exciting that kids didn't want to miss.

In our classroom-style Sunday school program, we began with a mini-worship service before the kids were dismissed to their classrooms. When they were dismissed, they would take the longest route possible to get to their classes. They needed to go to the restroom. They needed a drink of water. Any excuse was a good one, if it kept them out of the classroom a little longer. In our rotation-style learning program, we still begin with a mini-worship, but the kids have made it a foot race to get to the classrooms afterward. The excitement has barely diminished in the years since we started the program.

In rotation-style learning, the same material is reinforced in each of the labs over the course of a five- or six-week session. For instance, if we were doing a session on creation, the third graders might be in the art studio the first week doing an art project about creation. The second week, they might be in the computer lab putting together a multimedia retelling of the creation story, while the fourth graders are in the art studio. Over the course of a session, each class would spend one Sunday in each of the labs that are being used for that session.

## THE PUPPET LAB

In the puppetry room, the children learn by performing with puppets. It's not a puppet construction lab. It is strictly performance. We've used shadow puppets, rod puppets, marionettes, and even everyday objects as puppets. We use the same puppets and script for all the elementary grades, so the material has to work for first graders as well as sixth graders. In particular, the puppets have to work with the motor skills of even the youngest students.

Each Sunday morning in the puppet lab, we discuss the story, assign roles, rehearse the story, and videotape the final performance. The kids are given a great deal of room for creative input into how the story is performed. We use narration rather than dialog for the script, so the kids don't have lines to worry about and can focus on presenting the action and emotion of the story with their puppets.

## WHAT THIS BOOK IS ABOUT

This book is about using puppetry in a Sunday school classroom setting, but the ideas could easily be used in any classroom. We use puppetry to present stories from the Bible, but the same methods could just as easily be used to reinforce other types of stories.

Whether you are using rotation-style learning, classroom-style learning, or one-room schoolhouse-style learning in your Sunday school, puppetry is an extremely powerful tool for reinforcing the stories, bringing your kids into a deeper understanding of the stories, and for making the whole process of learning fun.

It's also important to understand what this book is not about. This book is not about bringing kids together as a "puppet team" to perform for audiences at church or community events. Over the past 20 or 30 years, many churches have

> *In the puppetry room, the children learn by performing with puppets.*

put together puppet teams and they have proven to be very effective, particularly as a form of outreach that actively involves kids.

## NEEDS AND GOALS

The needs and goals of a classroom puppetry program, as used in a rotation-style learning or traditional classroom, however, are very different from those of a puppet team. By necessity, a classroom program needs to use puppets that have very little learning curve. A child needs to be able to pick up a puppet for the first time at the beginning of a class and almost immediately feel comfortable using it. The bulk of the classroom time needs to be spent learning the story, not how to use the puppets.

The goal of our time in the puppetry room is to videotape the performance. It's a tangible goal that really gives the hour a focus. We are usually playing the video back for the kids at about the time the families are picking them up. The kids are both the performers and the audience for the puppet shows. It's a joy to see the creativity that's put into their performances and the pride that they have in the work that they have done.

A puppet team, on the other hand, needs to provide enough of a challenge that a commitment is involved and that improvement takes time. The moving-mouth puppets that most puppet teams use are very well suited to these needs. Lip synchronization (moving the puppet's mouth accurately with the spoken words) is not quickly mastered. Moving the puppet's arms and body realistically along with talking is an added challenge. A child (or adult) can spend a great deal of time becoming reasonably proficient with these moving-mouth, rod-arm puppets. Because of these challenges, moving-mouth puppets are not a particularly good choice of puppet for a classroom setting. Similarly, other puppets that are "just mouth," like sock puppets or paper bag puppets, are not recommended.

We've used a variety of styles of puppets that have worked very well with the children in our Sunday school program. It's been an enormously exciting process of discovery. We have learned a great deal through trial and error and, no doubt, will continue to learn more as we strive to find new ways to bring the stories of the Bible to life for our kids.

In this book I have tried to describe in detail what has worked well for us. I hope our ideas and methods will give you a solid place to begin. Other variations that you discover may be particularly well suited for your own program.

Whether you are using this book as a blueprint for a similar Sunday school program or as a source of ideas to add life to your existing program, I hope this book will help you discover what a powerful and delightful tool puppetry can be.

# Chapter 1

# The Case for Puppets in Christian Education

Puppetry is powerful. In a theatre, it can make things happen, physically and emotionally, that simply aren't possible any other way. In a therapy setting, puppetry can help break down emotional and psychological barriers. In the classroom, it can allow students to reach a new understanding of the stories they are learning and instill those stories through repetition. It can also foster teamwork as children and leaders work together toward a common goal. In a Sunday school setting, all of these strengths come into play.

Puppet use in the church is not a new idea. The earliest history of puppetry involves puppets being used to present the religious ideas of the day. The Christian church, in fact, is credited with the origin of the term "marionette." Puppets were so closely associated with nativity plays that the puppets became known as "little Marys" or "marionettes." For centuries, puppetry has been used as a tool to bring the stories of the Bible to life.

With puppets anything is possible. The epics of the Bible are tailor made for puppetry. Do you want to show the story of creation with dolphins swimming, birds flying, and horses galloping? It's possible. Do you want to cover the stage with a plague of locusts? It's possible. Do you need one child to perform as all of Joseph's brothers? It's all possible with puppetry.

> *With puppets anything is possible.*

Our Christian education director chose the life of Moses as the topic for our first unit. We covered the time from Moses' birth to the exodus from Egypt. Consequently, our drama included the basket among the reeds, the burning bush, the plagues, and the parting of the Red Sea. What would have been nearly impossible to do as a drama with human actors, was not difficult to put together with shadow puppets. God was clearly at work in those choices.

As a visual medium of limitless possibilities, puppetry is also a wonderful tool for biblical literacy. With the use of videotape, the kids are both performers and audience. They learn the story as they rehearse and perform, and the learning experience is capped as they watch their completed project on video. There is no better way to teach a story than through repetition; puppetry is a great way to make that repetition fun.

Another advantage of puppets in a Sunday school setting is the leveling effect that it has on the kids. Behind the puppet stage, the shyest kids will lose some of their inhibitions and perform with uncharacteristic boldness. Being hidden from view allows the child to focus completely on the puppet without worrying that they are being watched. I remember one particularly shy second-grade girl. She would hardly utter a word or look you in the eye. When she operated a

puppet, however, that character knew exactly where it had to go and what it had to do. Without it speaking a word, you knew exactly what the puppet was feeling.

The flip side of this effect comes into play with the most active and outgoing kids. Having to channel their energy through the puppet tends to dampen the energy that actually comes out in the performance. The puppet won't be as energetic as the child is.

Of course, there is also the general fascination that kids and adults have for puppets. (Adults just aren't given many opportunities to be fascinated, because so much of puppetry is aimed at kids.) This fascination is a wonderful way to draw them into the important stories of the Bible. Acting with a puppet and becoming a character in the story can draw a child into the story and give them a deeper understanding of how the characters felt and the importance of the story for our lives today.

*Behind the puppet stage, the shyest kids will lose some of their inhibitions and perform with uncharacteristic boldness.*

**Chapter 2** # Getting Started

The best advice that I can give you about getting started is to start small and plan ahead. Using puppets as a major teaching tool is a different way of working. For starters the energy levels will be different. When you first introduce puppets to the classroom, there will be an unusually high level of excitement among the kids. Keep this energy focused on learning and telling the story. High energy usually means the kids will have lots of ideas too. There will be wonderful ideas that add a special touch to the story. It may be an idea for something a puppet can do to help show how the puppet is feeling. It may be an idea for how the kids can work together to improve some part of the performance. There will also be ideas that have nothing to do with the story at hand. These ideas have to be politely dismissed. The leader should be able to keep things moving in the right direction with some "on topic" suggestions.

## TEACHING WITH PUPPETS

Teaching with puppets is different physically too. You won't be working with kids sitting in chairs around a table. At any point in time, some kids will be tucked behind the puppet stage figuring out their puppets and rehearsing, while other kids will be out front watching and waiting for their turn to perform. Between scenes the leaders will have to sort out which puppeteers are in the next scene, move some kids out of the stage and move some other kids in. Physically there will be a lot going on, probably a lot more than you are used to.

We always use two leaders or one leader and an aid. One suggestion is to use older kids as aids. One person demonstrates with the puppets, guides the discussion, and works with the kids backstage. The other person reads the narration, runs the video camera, and jumps in where necessary.

Of course, the puppets can't teach the story by themselves. It takes leaders who understand and relate well to the age level to create the cooperative atmosphere necessary for the kids to work effectively together to create a performance.

The point of starting small is primarily to give your leaders time to become comfortable with this new way of teaching. You should start with a small class too. Five or six kids is a good size. You will have enough kids to perform all the necessary roles for most stories, but you probably won't have to split a role between different kids to have enough for everyone to do.

Object theatre, which will be described in more detail in a later chapter, is the easiest way to get started, because it skips the step of building puppets and a

*Using puppets as a major teaching tool is a different way of working.*

stage. In this form of puppetry, household objects are used as puppets on a tabletop. Good objects for performing can be found at secondhand stores or in your own basement or attic. There's a sample script in a later chapter about the conversion of Saul that was written for object theatre.

If, after reading this book, you are especially excited about one of the other styles of puppetry, go ahead and follow that excitement. Shadow puppets or handle-bag puppets are also wonderful for getting started. Both of these types of puppets are easy to construct, but you will have to plan far enough ahead to allow time to get it done.

## USE YOUR RESOURCES

Your church probably has crafters, sewers, and carpenters who would be happy to help you create puppets, a stage, and curtains. These may be people who would love to help the Sunday school program, but who aren't interested in teaching. Put out the word in your church newsletter, make an announcement in church, or just ask around. These people shouldn't be hard to find. Only basic sewing and carpentry skills are required and the crafting skills can even be learned "on the job."

Any of the stages described later in this book would be a fairly simple project to hand off to a carpenter or person familiar with small building projects. Whomever you find to work on curtains may want to wait to begin their work until the stage is constructed to make sure that the curtains will fit properly. Planning ahead to allow enough time for this will be important. People work at different speeds, so let your volunteers tell you how long these projects will take.

Puppet construction works very well as a group project, but you should find a person to take the lead. Look for someone with craft skills. The leader will need to go over the construction instructions ahead of time, buy the materials, and probably make a sample puppet. A group of eight or 10 people will be able to make a complete set of handle-bag or shadow puppets in a four- to six-hour session.

## VIDEOTAPING

Whether you are starting with object theatre on a tabletop, or handle-bag puppets or shadow puppets on a more traditional stage, you will also need a video camera and a tripod. A television for playing the video is also very useful, but not absolutely necessary.

You will also need a room big enough to set up the camera far enough away from the stage that you will be able to get the whole playing area in the shot. We work in a room that is 14' x 17' (approx. 4 x 5 m). You wouldn't be able to work in a room much smaller than that. Ideally, you want to use a room that is big enough for your camera and stage, but not much bigger. If your classrooms are too small, you may be able to use part of a fellowship hall or multipurpose room.

*Your church probably has crafters, sewers, and carpenters who would be happy to help you create puppets, a stage, and curtains.*

Once you have your resources in place, get together with your teachers for a "dry run." Pull in some extra adults or a couple of kids too. Use the puppets and run through the story. This should give the teachers a clear picture of "what happens when" in the story and ideas about how it can be presented.

When you actually get to Sunday morning, the kids may have different ideas about how to present the story, but the leaders need to have suggestions ready for the inevitable time when the kids don't know what to do.

Once you get over the hump of getting started, it will be much easier to expand your program. Use your initial, experimental session for all your elementary grades. Work with your leaders to see what you need to do differently.

A month or two later, try another session with the same style of puppetry. When you're ready, try another style of puppetry. We use two or three different styles of puppetry to present three or four sessions each year. By mixing the styles of puppetry that we use, it stays exciting for the kids. We continue to present new stories, but after six years, we have the advantage of being able to repeat stories for a new group of elementary kids who weren't around to perform them the first time.

# Styles of Puppetry

# Chapter 3

The world of puppetry is blessed with an amazing diversity of styles. A puppet may be operated by rods, strings, cables or even radio control. If the puppet is controlled directly by the puppeteer, the puppeteer's hand, finger, foot, head or whole body may have to be used. A finger puppet may be a few inches tall and allow a puppeteer to operate a whole crowd of puppets at one time. A large parade puppet may be two or three times taller than the average person and require several puppeteers working very closely together. Different styles of puppetry have different strengths and work best in different settings.

We have found several styles of puppetry that work particularly well in the Sunday school classroom. I'm sure there are other styles we haven't explored that could work equally well.

## SHADOW PUPPETS

When we were adding puppetry to our Sunday school program, I decided that we would use shadow puppetry for the first unit. The decision was a pragmatic one. We had a puppet stage to build with curtains and lights and I wanted to minimize the amount of time we would spend building puppets. Shadow puppets are flat figures that can be made from poster board rather quickly, so they seemed like a good choice.

I recently found out that when I told our Christian education director that we would be using shadow puppets, she was terribly disappointed. I think she was hoping for something more exciting. The special magic of shadow puppetry won her over, however, when she actually saw the puppets in action. The puppets had the same effect on the kids.

Although most of our kids had never seen a shadow puppet before, they took to them immediately. There's a certain charm about shadow puppets that appeals to young and old alike. On page 12 are images of some of the shadow puppets that we used to tell the life of Moses.

For the life of Moses, we used different sizes of puppets for different scenes. Small puppets were used for Moses and the Hebrew people in the "parting of the Red Sea" scene, so the people would be small compared to the Red Sea. In the scenes between Moses and Pharaoh, larger puppets were used.

The shadow puppets that we use are quite simple. Most are made from black poster board and have no moving parts. When necessary, we have used colored tissue paper to add color. The fire for the burning bush, for instance, was done this way.

*Because they are simple, shadow puppets can be constructed quite quickly. They are flat and therefore easy to store.*

## Moses and the Hebrew People

Moses

Pharaoh

*Moses Shadow Puppets*

Because they are simple, shadow puppets can be constructed quite quickly. They are flat and therefore easy to store. About the only disadvantage to shadow puppets is that they are usually created for a specific story and generally aren't easily reusable for different stories.

To perform with shadow puppets, you need a light source and a shadow screen. The shadow screen consists of fabric or another material stretched over a frame. You can't see through the shadow screen, but when a shadow puppet is placed on the back of the screen, between the screen and the light source, you see the shadow cast by the puppet.

The puppets are operated from behind by rods made of wire. Most of our puppets just have one rod, but if a puppet has one or more moving parts, it may need a second rod.

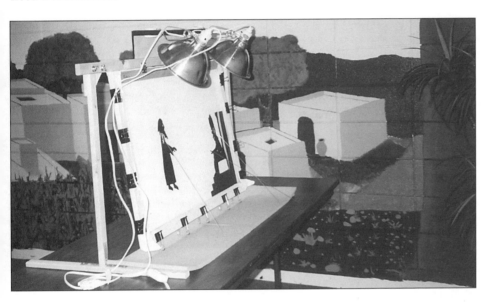

*Shadow Screen Set-up*

Unless you are using a very focused source of light, like an overhead projector, the puppets have to be touching the screen or the shadow will be fuzzy. The farther the puppet is from the screen, the fuzzier the shadow gets. The puppet should be held lightly on the screen. If it is pushed against the screen too hard, the screen may be stretched and the puppet may be bent. If a puppet is bent, it won't lie flat against the screen and part of the shadow will always be fuzzy.

Since the puppets have to slide along the screen to move, they are usually moved rather slowly. Moving the puppets slowly also makes them easier to see.

Scenery can be made from poster board, just like the puppets, and tucked between the frame of the shadow screen and the screen material. The more scenery you have, however, the less room you will have on the screen for the puppets to perform.

If the top of the screen is tipped slightly toward the audience, the shadow puppet can be left resting on the screen supported by the control rod. A sheet of ½" (12 mm) thick foam rubber, 10"-12" (25-30 cm) wide and as long as the

screen, set behind the shadow screen, will keep the rods from sliding and hold the shadow puppet against the screen. If you have more puppets that need to be "on stage" than you have room for puppeteers, it can be very helpful to leave a puppet resting on the screen.

## HANDLE-BAG PUPPETS

The handle-bag puppet is a style of rod puppet developed especially for use with children by George Latshaw, an innovative and brilliant puppeteer, director, designer, and educator and an enormously generous man. While George was working as an Artist-in-the-Schools for the Ohio Arts Council and Young Audiences of Greater Cleveland, Inc., the grade level for school residencies in puppetry dropped from fifth grade to kindergarten. It was a disconcerting development for a man who wanted to share his art in as sophisticated a form as possible. The prospect of stick puppets or paper-bag "talkers" was not encouraging. As George puts it, "I wanted children to experience puppets that could *do* things, not just run their mouths and bob their heads with crackling paper dialog." This challenge led him to develop the handle-bag puppet.

*Handle-Bag Puppet*

Each handle-bag puppet consists simply of a head on a short handle rod and a fabric bag for a body. The handle on the head goes through a hole in the center of the bag. One hand holds the head handle and the other hand, placed in a corner of the bag, becomes the puppet's hand. It's an enormously simple puppet, but also enormously effective.

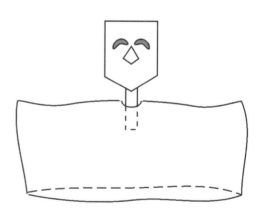

*Basic Handle-Bag Puppet*

Because the child's hand becomes the puppet's hand, these puppets can gesture and handle props very easily. There is practically no learning curve involved in operating a handle-bag puppet, which makes them ideal for the classroom.

*A basic set of handle-bag puppet characters can be used and reused in many different stories.*

Because the bag for the body is not attached to the head, a costume change is simply a matter of slipping the head handle into a new bag. When we did the story of Joseph, he had three costumes: his multicolored coat, a ragged slave costume, and an expensive looking "Pharaoh's right-hand man" costume. The costume changes were so easy that the kids took care of them by themselves as the story went along.

A basic set of handle-bag puppet characters can be used and reused in many different stories. Consequently, these puppets have really become the backbone of our program.

Handle-bag puppets can perform on the simplest of stages. Because they handle props well, we always use a stage with a playboard. A playboard is a small shelf on the front of the stage where the puppets can set props. It should be 4"-6" (10-15 cm) deep and as wide as the stage opening. Scenery can also be attached to the playboard.

The puppeteers standing behind the stage can either operate the puppets overhead or at head level, if you're using a stage with a scrim-type backdrop. A scrim is a loosely woven fabric backdrop that the puppeteers can see through from behind. If it is lit from the front, but not the back, you won't be able to see the puppeteers. Our stage has fabric over the top and back as well to make sure that light doesn't come through the back of the scrim.

Using a scrim allows the puppeteers to see the puppets from the back rather than from below. It also makes it easier for puppeteers of different heights to work side-by-side.

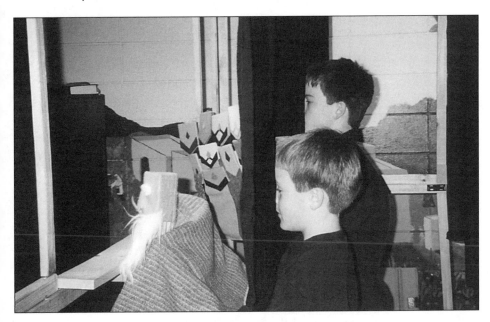

*Operating Behind Scrim*

When introducing handle-bag puppets to the kids for the first time, you'll need to help them learn how to operate the puppets. George Latshaw has suggested a very effective way to do this. The teacher teaches the puppet how to

move. Have one child take one of the puppet heads without the body. The teacher uses his or her own head to nod "yes" or shake "no." The teacher looks up at the ceiling and then down at the floor. Have the puppet repeat each of these moves. Now slip the handle through the neck of the bag. Have the child slip his or her other hand into the far corner of the bag. Now the puppet can wave, cover the mouth to cough, stretch for a yawn, pick up props, and so on.

The child can use either hand, right or left, as the hand of the puppet. The child can even switch hands at any time by passing the head rod to the other hand.

## MARIONETTES

My favorite style of puppet is the marionette, so I'll admit to a certain amount of bias. Marionettes are not especially difficult to operate, although construction of them is more difficult than for other forms of puppetry. Adults tend to have a fear-of-tangling phobia about marionettes, but children don't tend to suffer from this. We've used our marionettes successfully both in our own church and in other churches that we've helped get started using puppetry.

I have to admit, though, that the difficulties of constructing marionettes will put them out of the reach of most churches. It is also beyond the scope of this book to cover marionette construction in enough detail to serve as a practical starting point. If, after all the disclaimers, you are still interested in marionettes, contact me directly and I will be more than happy to help you get started. I can be contacted through my Web page (www.HunterMarionettes.com).

## OBJECT THEATRE

When we started our puppetry program, the goal was simply to serve the children of our church with the highest quality program that we could. The complexity of the puppets wasn't an issue. We could use anything that I could design and build. After the first couple of years, though, we found ourselves in the position of working with other churches as they began similar programs. Consequently, I began looking for simpler methods that could be used in a puppetry program. One of the simplest methods is to use household objects as puppets. Although not well known by the general public, there is a very strong movement in the world of puppetry known as "object theatre."

Anyone who has ever enacted a dinner-table drama with salt and pepper shakers has a general idea of object theatre. Ideally, the objects cast in this type of a tabletop drama will have logical relationships with the roles they are playing. I remember a professional performance, for instance, where half-pint milk cartons were used as cows. In this same show, the seeds that the farmer planted were dice rolled out of a cup, making a subtle connection to the inherent risks of farming.

When we've used object theatre, we've let the kids do the casting, deciding which objects to use for which characters. It's been interesting to see the connections that they have made between the objects and the characters.

*Anyone who has ever enacted a dinner-table drama with salt and pepper shakers has a general idea of object theatre.*

Probably the greatest advantage of object theatre is that there are no puppets to construct. The objects used can be found at garage sales, secondhand stores, or in your own basement or garage. Although object theatre is quite easy to pull together, it's also very popular with the kids. Since they are making all the decisions of what objects to use for the various characters and props, they have more ownership of the final product.

The extra decision-making responsibility that the kids have leads to some extra responsibilities for the teachers too. There will be conflicting ideas between the kids. The teachers have to be the guides who bring everyone to common ground. The teachers also have to handle continuity issues. For instance, if the pink plastic bottle is Joshua in the first scene, then that bottle should be Joshua for the rest of the story. The teachers should keep track of the needs of the whole story. If you only have one object that can work as the ark of the covenant, then you have to steer the kids away from using that object as the chief priest earlier in the story.

We have staged object theatre in two different ways. For our variation of the parable of the good Samaritan—we call it "The Good Spatula"—all the characters are tools or kitchen utensils: a cheese grater, hammers, a ladle, and so forth. For this story, we use a traditional puppet stage with the utensils being operated as puppets from below.

Most object theatre, however, is done on a tabletop. Normally puppeteers in tabletop drama would be in view of the audience at the back of the table. However, since one of the advantages of puppetry in the classroom is that the child doesn't have to be seen, we've tried to stage our tabletop dramas so that the puppeteers don't show up on the videotape.

We have set up a small scrim backdrop at the back of the table that hangs down to 3"-4"(8-10 cm) above the table. The child can reach under the scrim to operate the objects, while looking through the scrim. The majority of the puppeteering, however, is done by reaching in from the sides of the table. The kids always have to be reminded that they have to stay behind the edges of the table to stay out of the scene and avoid getting between the puppets and the video camera. They tend to get wrapped up in the story and forget where the camera is.

Since the objects in general don't have moving parts, the manipulation of the objects has more to do with how the objects are leaning, how fast they are moving, and the way they are moving. Think about how you would have a salt shaker walk, if it were depressed or excited or mad. How would a very proud salt shaker walk versus a very shy one? If the answers to these questions aren't immediately clear to you, then check with a kid. They have no trouble seeing a salt shaker as a little woman and know exactly how she would walk if she were happy.

*Ideas for object theatre puppets:*
- *cheese grater*
- *spatula*
- *hammer*
- *salt and pepper shakers*
- *ladle*
- *milk cartons*

## OTHER OPTIONS

Masks have a lot of potential for use in Sunday school dramas. A simple, hand-held mask can be made from pantyhose and a coat hanger. Bend the body of the coat hanger into a face-shaped oval. Bend the hook into a loop. This loop will be the handle. Slide a leg from the pantyhose over the oval of wire and tie it off at the top and bottom. You now have the basis for a mask that you can see through. Add features and hair with felt and fake fur and you are ready to go. Masks have the advantage of hiding the child, yet leaving them with their whole body for performing.

Another method for presenting shadow puppetry is to work with an overhead projector. The puppets have to be smaller, but you don't need a special shadow screen, and the scenery can be drawn on transparencies.

The possibility of combining a craft project with a puppet performance project is another idea that we haven't had a chance to explore yet. Shadow puppets or handle-bag puppet heads could be created by the kids in Sunday school over a few weeks. The final Sunday of the project would be rehearsing and videotaping a performance with the puppets. The schedule would have to be planned carefully to ensure that there was sufficient time to get the puppets built. Too often in a classroom setting, puppet construction consumes all the scheduled time and the finished puppets never see a performance.

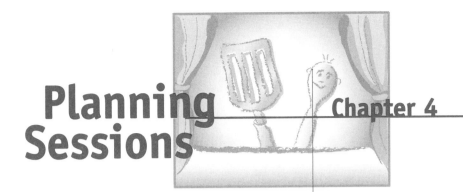

# Planning Sessions

# Chapter 4

## CHOOSING THE PUPPETRY STYLE FOR THE STORY

Choosing the best style of puppet for the story or deciding whether puppets are well suited for the story at all is the first step in planning a session. Usually, our Christian education director will talk to us about the units that are planned for the year and we will decide which ones lend themselves to puppetry. In general, a story needs action and emotion to give the puppets something to do. Without clear things for the puppets to do, a puppet performance will never get off the ground.

If puppets seem like a good choice to tell the story, then the next decision is which kind of puppets will work best. If the story requires the characters to handle props, then handle-bag puppets may be the best choice. If the story involves a lot of animals or epic scenes, such as the story of creation, then shadow puppets or object theatre would be a better choice. I always picture in my mind how a story could be presented with the various kinds of puppets to help me make my choice.

If you're not a person who is comfortable visualizing, then try checking out the story hands-on. Grab some glasses from your cupboard and anything else you have handy, walk them around, and see if object theatre can be used to tell your story. If you have some handle-bag puppets, try using them. If you don't have handle-bag puppets, then just pretend that you do. Wad up a piece of newspaper and hold it in one hand as a puppet head. Use your other hand as the puppet's hand. Try acting out the story. Play all the roles yourself.

If you think shadow puppets might work, then think about what puppets you would need and what they would do. Make a list of all the puppets and scenery you would need to tell the story. If you're still not sure, then draw a little picture of each scene. Stick figures will work fine.

To give you a rough idea of what can be done, following are some units that we have presented with different styles of puppetry.

*If puppets seem like a good choice to tell the story, then the next decision is which kind of puppets will work best.*

| STORY | PUPPETRY STYLE |
|---|---|
| The Life of Moses | Shadow Puppets |
| Creation | Shadow Puppets |
| Joseph the Dreamer | Handle-Bag Puppets (plus shadow puppets for the dreams) |
| Abraham and Sarah | Handle-Bag Puppets |
| Jacob and Esau | Handle-Bag Puppets |
| Kind, Blind Bartimaeus | Marionettes |
| Saul Sees the Light | Object Theatre |
| Joshua and the Walls of Jericho | Object Theatre |

## SCRIPT WRITING

One of the keys to the way that we've put our stories together is that our puppets don't talk. More specifically, the kids don't speak for the puppets. With less than an hour to rehearse and videotape a story, the kids have more than enough to do performing the action of the story with their puppets.

Our stories are told by a narrator, who may be a teacher or one of the kids. If we're working with one of the younger grades, a teacher will read the narration. If there are good readers in the class, we'll have one of them read the narration.

In general, the script needs to be as simple and direct as possible. It should be little more than a skeleton to direct the action of the story. You want to avoid sections of narration that don't give the puppets anything to do. You should also be sure to specifically include all the necessary action in the script. For instance, in one script we needed Joseph's brothers to exit after Joseph told them about his dreams. The original script just said "Joseph's brothers were very mad" and then we tried to have the kids remember to have the brothers leave. It worked much better when we changed the narration to "Joseph's brothers got very mad and left."

We have always used Bible stories, so the Bible is always my starting point. As I read through the story, I will note the actions and emotions of the characters. Those are really the two things that the script needs to contain. Frequently, the original Bible story will contain more action and details than we can include in a three- to five-minute drama. The decisions about what to skip will usually be based on what particular ideas we are trying to emphasize.

Occasionally, a story will need to be fleshed out with details that are not found in the Bible, so that there is enough material for a drama. When we used the story of blind Bartimaeus, we added the character of a girl who helped Bartimaeus find his way to Jesus.

You will also need to keep in mind the style of puppet that you will be using when you write the script. Make sure that the action you write into the script is possible with the puppets you will be using. If you're not sure what is possible

*Frequently, the original Bible story will contain more action and details than we can include in a three- to five-minute drama.*

with the puppets, get out some puppets and give it a try. Nothing will clarify what actually works in a script better than having some puppets run through it.

One other thing to keep in mind when preparing the script is how many and how few kids you can expect to have in the classroom on a given Sunday. Can the script be performed if you have only three kids? Are there enough roles if you have 15 kids? If the story takes place in multiple locations, we will usually break it up into multiple scenes. As a general rule, each location will be a different scene. You may also need to split a story into different scenes, if the story jumps ahead in time. If we need to, we can use a different group of kids for each scene to ensure that everyone has a role.

Below is the script that we used for the story of the conversion of Saul. For this particular story, we used object theatre. As you read through the script, picture how the story would be performed using objects operated on a tabletop. If visualizing doesn't work for you, gather some objects and try acting out the story.

*How many and how few kids can you expect to have in the classroom on a given Sunday?*

### Script—Paul Sees the Light

#### *SCENE 1*

A long, long time ago, when the Christian church was just starting, the followers of Jesus, the Christians, preached wherever they could. On street corners or in the temples, they would talk about Jesus to anyone who would listen.

Not everyone believed the Christians when they said that Jesus was the son of God. Many Jews believed that the Christians were preaching terrible lies. One of these Jews was a man named Saul. He tried very hard to be a good Jew and to do what God wanted him to.

Saul would get very mad when he heard the Christians preaching. "The lies must be stopped," he thought.

He went to the temple and talked to the chief priest. He got permission from the priest to send any Christians that he found to prison.

#### *SCENE 2*

Saul sent many Christians to prison in Jerusalem. Soon the Christians were very frightened of him.

Saul wouldn't stop with Jerusalem. He decided to go to the city of Damascus to stop the Christians there too.

#### *SCENE 3*

Saul took some friends with him and they started the long walk to Damascus. Suddenly there was a brilliant light from the sky. Saul fell to the ground in terror. A voice said, "Saul, Saul, why do you persecute me?"

"Who are you?" Saul asked weakly.

"I am Jesus, whom you are persecuting," said the voice. "Go on to the city and you will be told what you are to do."

Saul's friends were shocked. They had heard the voice, but saw no one there. Saul got up from the ground. He opened his eyes, but he could see nothing. The other men led Saul on to Damascus to the house where he would stay.

### SCENE 4

For three days, Saul couldn't eat or drink. He spent most of his time praying.

In Damascus there was also a Christian man named Ananias. God spoke to Ananias and told him to go to Saul. Ananias had heard of the terrible things that Saul had done to other Christians. He didn't want to go to Saul, but God said that he had great plans for Saul, so Ananias did what God asked him to do.

When Ananias met Saul, he told him that Jesus had sent him so that Saul's sight would be restored and he would be filled with God's spirit. Immediately, Saul could see again. Saul was amazed.

### SCENE 5

Saul wanted to be baptized right away, so they went to the river and Ananias baptized Saul.

Now Saul couldn't stop talking about Jesus. He was as excited about Jesus now He told everyone he saw what had happened to him and that Jesus was the son of God.

Everyone who knew him was amazed. They couldn't believe that this was the same person who had been sending Christians to prison.

### SCENE 6

The Jews that had helped Saul against the Christians couldn't believe what had happened. They plotted to kill Saul and watched the city gates day and night to make sure he couldn't escape.

The Christians heard about these plans against Saul and came up with their own plan. They lowered Saul over the city wall in a basket and he escaped and returned to Jerusalem.

### SCENE 7

From Jerusalem, Saul traveled all over the world teaching about Jesus. And from then on he was called Paul, because he was not the same man any more.

## PREPARING PUPPETS, PROPS, AND STAGE.

Once your script is complete, you should have a good idea of what puppets, props, and staging you will need to tell your story. If the story has become too complicated, involving many puppets or props that you don't already have, you may want to take another look at the script to see how it can be simplified and still maintain the message that you are hoping to get across.

If you are telling a new story with handle-bag puppets, there may be props or puppets you don't have that are vital to the story. If this is the case, talk to

*Once your script is complete, you should have a good idea of what puppets, props, and staging you will need to tell your story.*

your craft people again. You probably have someone in your church who would love the challenge of making David's harp or Joseph's multicolored coat.

If you are using shadow puppets, you may want to find someone in your congregation with some graphic talent to draw puppet patterns for you. Great artistic talent and experience isn't required. Show them some of the shadow puppet designs from this book. You probably have someone who can do just as well or better.

If you are using object theatre to tell your story, you need to be sure that the story can be told with the objects that you have. When we did the story of Joshua at Jericho, we had to supplement our set of objects with boxes and other things that could be used as Jericho's wall.

## SUPPORTING YOUR LEADERS

Sunday school leaders always appreciate a session plan that includes specific details about the story being told or the puppets being used. I will usually include questions or topics for discussion to introduce the story, as well as specific details about the puppets being used that need to be reinforced. Below is a sample session plan for the story of the conversion of Saul.

### Session Plan—Paul Sees the Light

#### 1. Attendance

Begin each session by having each of the kids sign their names on the cardstock 11" x 17" (28 x 43 cm) credits sheet underneath the heading "Starring." Use a new cardstock sheet for each Sunday. When you videotape the story at the end of the class, videotape the credits sheet before videotaping anything else.

#### 2. Reading and Discussing the Story

With the kids seated in a circle, ask them whether they have heard of Paul. What do they know about him?

Have they heard of Saul?

Read the story to them or have them take turns reading.

Ask them what they think is important about the story. Discuss their ideas. Let them know what you think is important about the story. Here are some things you could discuss:

Was it difficult to be a Christian during that time? Is it difficult to be a Christian today?

How does God talk to you? Does God ask you to do things that you don't want to do?

#### 3. Object Theatre Instructions

Explain to the kids that they will be deciding how to use the objects to tell the story. They have to decide which objects to use for each of the characters and props.

Explain to the kids that the objects should be put back on the table when they are not being used in a scene.

### 4. Rehearsal

Read through the story one scene at a time and decide what objects to use and who will be performing each character. After you've read through a scene and assigned all the roles, rehearse it with the narration. The narrator needs to constantly watch the puppets and wait for them. It's very easy for the narration to go too fast and get way ahead of the actions of the puppets.

When the kids are deciding which objects to use, you will need to make sure that the object used for Paul will fit in the basket. It is the only object that will work for lowering Paul over the city walls.

For the road to Damascus scene, there is a clip light that can be turned on at the appropriate moment to represent the bright light in the sky.

### 5. Videotaping

It will probably work best with this story to rehearse a scene and then video-tape it before moving on to the next scene. Don't forget to start by videotaping the credits.

### 6. Playback

After you have videotaped all the scenes, hook the video camera to the television and play the completed story for the kids. If the worship service hasn't finished yet, when you are done playing the video, play it again. The kids usually enjoy seeing it more than once.

A session plan isn't enough if a leader is new to the puppet room or new to the style of puppet that's being used. Teaming a new leader with an experienced leader is the best way to bring a new leader up to speed. Have the experienced leader take the lead for the first Sunday or two, so the new leader can get a feel for how the room works. On the second or third Sunday, have the new leader take the lead, while the experienced leader plays the secondary role and serves as a safety net.

If you are just starting out with a new style of puppetry, you might want to hold an evening workshop. Gather your leaders together to explore the new puppets together. Play with the puppets. Explore what they can and can't do.

It's important to remember that you don't need any prior experience with puppets to teach in this puppetry program. Because the puppets must be very easy for the kids to learn to operate, they will also be easy for the leaders to learn. It's a good point to remember when recruiting leaders. The leaders have the added benefit of being able to work with the puppets and the story before Sunday morning until they are thoroughly comfortable with both.

# A Typical Sunday Morning

# Chapter 5

## THE SET-UP

Our Sunday school is set up based on the rotation-style learning model, so we have a room that is only used for puppetry. The centerpiece of our "Parable Productions" room is the puppet stage. Next to the stage is a long table where the puppets are laid out when they are not being used. The only other things you will find in the room are a video camera on a tripod and a television set sitting on the top of a cabinet.

If you are working in a classroom-style arrangement, you will probably be moving the puppet stage and video camera from one learning space to another as needed. If you don't have a television in the classroom, you may be able to take the kids and the camera to a television at the end of class time to watch the tape.

In a traditional classroom setting, the puppets could easily be used as a special session that takes the entire class time for one Sunday. If you are studying a particular story for several weeks, the puppets could be used on the first Sunday to plant the story firmly in their minds. You could also use the puppets on the last Sunday as a special way of wrapping up the session. In any of those situations, you would present the class in the same manner that will be described below.

We usually have two leaders in the room, so that one can read the narration and operate the video camera, while the other works behind the puppet stage with the kids. If we have a new leader working with the puppets, we will usually have that leader operating the camera and reading the narration. That is an easier role to play, while learning the dynamics of the room.

Before the kids arrive, you will need to make sure that the video camera is set up. You should also make sure that you have the cables to connect the camera to the television, if you are using an 8mm camera. The details of videotaping are included later in this chapter.

## ARRIVAL

The first thing the children do when they come into the room is to sign in on our credits board. The credits board has the name of the story and a place for the kids to add their own names. When we get to the point of videotaping, we videotape the credits board first, so it appears as the opening title and credits for the video.

Over the years, we have tried doing the credits board in a variety of ways. We have used a small whiteboard, a sign board with removable lettering, and sheets designed on the computer and printed on 11" x 17" (28 x 43 cm) cardstock as our credits board.

The whiteboard worked well, but didn't look particularly professional on the video. The sign board with the removable lettering looked very good, but it took a long time for the kids to sign in—they had to find all the letters to spell out their name from the tray of letters and then get them placed on the sign. The cardstock sheets look good and also allow the kids to quickly sign in. As you may have guessed, the credits board is also our way of taking attendance. See page 63 in the appendix for a sample credits sheet to use or adapt to fit your needs.

Because there are no chairs in the room, we gather the kids in a circle on the floor as soon as they have signed in. We begin by talking about the story that we will be performing. After some discussion about the story, we will read through the script and show them the puppets that they will be using to tell the story. If there are good readers in the class, we will have them take turns, each reading a paragraph of the script, as we show the puppets and explain the action of the story. For the younger children, one of the leaders will read while the other demonstrates the puppets.

There are usually special instructions that need to be mentioned about the specific type of puppet being used (such as a reminder that shadow puppets are very fragile.) It's also helpful to give examples of the actions and emotions that will come into play in the story as you read through the script. The examples can help get ideas flowing.

## REHEARSAL

Assigning the roles for the story always needs to be handled carefully. The kids can have strong ideas about who they want to be in the story. The excitement level can be pretty high at this point and feelings can easily be hurt. Assigning roles is more art than science and depends a lot on how well the leader knows the kids in the class. However you decide to do this, make sure there is rotation and variation in the way roles are chosen or assigned.

Occasionally, we will have a child who doesn't want to perform in the story. Our approach has been to respect the child's wishes. If the child is simply uncomfortable with the idea of performing and isn't acting out, it isn't a problem. Pushing a child to perform who isn't comfortable doesn't help the child or the group effort. They will still be involved in the discussion of the story and will watch the rehearsals with the kids that aren't involved in the scene being rehearsed. At any point in the process, there will usually be other kids watching the rehearsal of a scene that they are not involved in. They will still be involved in the "learning by seeing," but they will miss the "learning by doing." Sometimes the child will later change their mind and we will rearrange things as best we can to give them a small role.

Our stories tend to be divided into three or four scenes, and we rehearse the story scene by scene. If a child is not involved in the scene being rehearsed, he or

she is expected to be sitting in front of the puppet stage watching the rehearsal. Similarly, if a puppet is not involved in a scene, it is expected to be on the puppet table. We emphasize the idea that the puppets are not toys. They are for performing. If they are not in the current scene, they should be on the puppet table. Because the puppets we use are not children's toys, we don't have a problem with the kids seeing them as toys.

One reason that the children take these simple puppet performances seriously is that we take them seriously. The leader very much sets the tone for the room. If the leader approaches this as play time, then play is what the kids will focus on. They won't be focusing on the story being told. If, however, the leader keeps the energy focused on the story, amazing things can happen.

As a general rule, the learners themselves should be deciding how to present the action and emotion of the story. They are much more likely to remember the story if they are plotting their own path. If the kids are coming up with the ideas, the leader only needs to keep the action appropriate to the story and keep things moving from scene to scene.

If the kids are having trouble with ideas, it may just take a gentle reminder from the leader—"Jacob is really sad now"—to point a child in the right direction. Sometimes a more direct tactic will be necessary, if a child isn't staying focused on the story. In these situations, the leader may have to suggest very specific actions for the puppets: "Okay, Jacob hugs Joseph now. Maybe they're jumping for joy too."

It can also very easy for leaders to get so involved in the process of directing, that they don't leave much room for the creativity of the children. At its best, the puppet play is a collaborative process between the children and the leaders. The children are offering suggestions to the leaders and to each other. The leaders are offering suggestions, when necessary, and guiding the final decision.

We will usually rehearse the entire story twice before videotaping. If the story is long or if there's not enough time for some other reason, one rehearsal will do. If the story is particularly complicated, we will sometimes rehearse a scene and videotape it before moving on to the next scene.

> *As a general rule, the learners themselves should be deciding how to present the action and emotion of the story.*

## VIDEOTAPING

The goal of each Sunday school session, the videotaping of the story, is another reason why the kids take it seriously. I can't overemphasize the importance of the videotaping. It gives the room a sense of purpose that I never would have expected. Even if the children seem to be completely unfocused during the rehearsals, they quickly become quiet and focused for the videotaping.

The first rule of videotaping is that everyone has to be completely quiet, so the narration can be heard on the videotape. Even with everyone quiet, the narrator needs to remember to stay close to the camera, so the narration will be picked up clearly. We do a 3-2-1 countdown so that everyone knows when the taping has started.

We only tape each scene once. If something goes wrong, there's usually no time to go back and tape it again. Looking back, I'm a little surprised that this hasn't been a problem. There are frequently small things that go wrong, but rarely anything that gets in the way of continuing with the story. The glitches can add a certain charm or at least comic relief to the story.

We end the hour by playing the completed video back for the kids. Although the videotaping has proven to be a very important element, the playback has proven to be much less important. For our first full year, in fact, we didn't have any means of playing the video back for the kids at the end of the hour. Toward the end of the first year, some of the kids figured out that I could see the video through the eyepiece of the camera, as I fast forwarded and rewound the tape. From this discovery, the kids devised their own way of watching the playback. They would patiently stand in line to get their 20-second turn at the eyepiece as the story played (in black and white and without sound).

We have rarely used the videotapes for anything other than playback at the end of the hour. When we were starting the new Sunday school program, we used the tapes once or twice during a potluck meal or other special event. We didn't showed the tapes to a large group, but we would have a tape running in the puppetry room, so that people could stop in and get an idea of what we were doing. We have talked about compiling videotapes of the year's performances for each grade, but it's an idea that we've never followed up on.

We are usually playing the tape at about the time the families are coming to pick up their kids, so the kids take the opportunity to give their parents a running commentary on their involvement in the performance. We will sometimes have to do a second showing to allow a particular parent to see his or her child's performance. To see the pride that the children take in their performances is truly a joy.

### Videotaping Tips

The video camera that we use is an 8mm video camcorder. Other possibilities would have been VHS or compact VHS. In our case, the decision was an easy one. Our church already owned a 8mm camcorder, so that's what we use. There are advantages and disadvantages to each type of camera. The greatest advantage of a VHS camera is that you can pop your tape into any VCR for viewing. This would be a definite advantage if you don't have a television in the room where you will be videotaping, but do have a television somewhere else. Rather than taking the camera to the television, you just need to take the tape. Also, VHS lets you avoid the potential hassle of connecting a cable between your 8mm camera and your television and getting the two to behave properly together. The main disadvantage of a VHS camcorder is simply the size.

Compact VHS (VHS-C) camcorders also have the advantage of being able to use any VCR for playback. You will need a VHS-C adapter, however. Compact VHS camcorders are also smaller and lighter than full-sized VHS camcorders.

The real advantages of 8mm camcorders are better sound quality and the ability to record longer on one tape. Since the puppet dramas seldom go much

> *To see the pride that the children take in their performances is truly a joy.*

more than five minutes, neither of these advantages make much difference in the puppet room. These advantages do, however, make 8mm camcorders very popular, so you probably have lots of potential Sunday school leaders in your church who are familiar with 8mm cameras.

If you are using an 8mm camera, refer to your camcorder instruction manual for the correct way to connect your camera to a television or VCR.

If you do have a television available in the room where you are rehearsing and performing, you might be tempted to have the camera connected to the television while the camera is on. I thought that would be a great idea. I figured it would let the kids see, while they were rehearsing and performing, what the performance would look like. On the contrary, it turned out to be a big distraction. There was always someone waving a hand in front of the camera or making faces, so they could watch it on the television. For the same reason, we use the eyepiece, not the LCD display, on our camera.

For most styles of puppet performances, the camera should be at the same height as the puppets and framed so that you are videotaping just a little wider than the area where the puppets will be. If you are taping a tabletop drama, however, it works better to have the camera higher than the tabletop, so that you can angle down slightly and see the entire tabletop. This allows the objects/puppets to use much more of the table and still be seen.

After we have framed the shot, so that all the puppets will be seen, we don't zoom or move the camera. Since one leader is operating the camera and also reading the narration, it really isn't possible.

When taping shadow puppet performances, we have had some trouble leaving the camera on autofocus. Trying to focus on the bright shadow lights, the camera may continually focus in and out just a little bit. If this happens, you should try putting the camera on manual focus. You will need to focus the camera once before you start shooting, but you shouldn't have to worry about it after that.

## Chapter 6 Stages

There are multiple ways you can build a puppet stage. My first puppet stage, many years ago, was made out of the large cardboard box from the new church organ. It worked wonderfully while performances were only presented in our basement. After our first show "on the road" at a church out in the country, we realized that hauling a big cardboard box in the back of a pick-up truck wasn't the easiest way to go. Since then, I've gone through many different stages, all with their advantages and disadvantages.

The most basic requirement for a puppet stage is that it allows the puppets to be seen while hiding the puppeteers. For handle-bag puppets, this requirement can be satisfied with any sort of a simple screen. Each type of puppetry, however, will also have additional requirements.

### SHADOW-PUPPET STAGE

The heart of a shadow-puppet stage is the shadow screen. A shadow-puppet stage will also need to have a light source and masking to hide the puppeteers. The stage described in this section is designed to sit on a table.

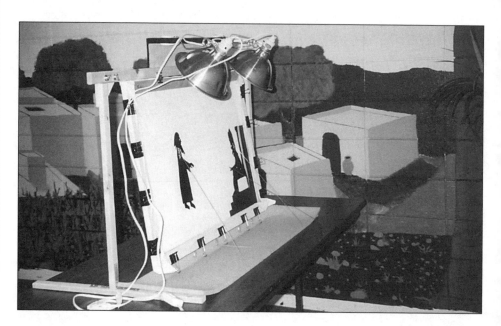

*Shadow-Puppet Stage*

## Shadow-Puppet Stage Materials

➤ Artists' precut frame pieces: Artists use these to make frames to stretch canvas over. They are available at art or craft supply stores, and may be labeled as "stretch strips." We purchased four pieces—two 2' (60 cm) lengths and two 3' (90 cm) lengths—to construct a 2' x 3' (60 x 90 cm) shadow screen.

➤ White plastic shower curtain liner: We use this to cover the shadow screen. It's a smooth surface for the puppets to slide across and it does a good job of diffusing the light.

➤ Large binder clips: You should be able to find these clips, usually used for holding large unbound documents, at an office supply store. The clips that fit our frame are listed as "clip size 2 inches (5 cm), capacity 1⅛ inches (28 mm)". You will use them to hold the shower curtain onto the wooden frame, so the clips need to be big enough to fit over the frame. The clips work very well because you can tighten the shadow screen if it stretches.

➤ Thumb tacks: Used to attach the screen to the frame at the top edge only, where the screen attaches to the support frame.

➤ Clamp lights with 8½" (22 cm) metal reflectors: You will need two of these to cover a 2' x 3' (60 x 90 cm) screen. Use 150-watt bulbs, or the highest wattage bulb that the clamp light is rated for. The lights should be attached at the top of the screen and aimed down onto the screen.

➤ Wood glue: For assembling the shadow screen and constructing the frame support.

➤ Lumber: (1" x 2"/2.5 x 5 cm pine) For the support frame.

➤ Plywood: (¼"/6 mm) For the support frame.

➤ Metal angle braces: For the support frame. You'll need four of these.

➤ Slip hinges: You'll need two of these to attach the screen to the support frame. A slip hinge is similar to a loose pin hinge, except that the pin is permanently attached to one side of the hinge and fits loosely into the other half. Loose pin hinges can also be used.

➤ Bolts, wing-nuts, and washers: ( ¼"/6 mm) You'll need four of each of these to allow support frame to be dismantled for storage.

➤ Assorted screws and brads: For attaching plywood and angle braces.

➤ Hook-and-loop fasteners: (1"/2.5 cm wide) To attach curtain to stage.

➤ Fabric: For the stage curtain. Lightweight crushed velvet or robe velour, which has a velvet look to it but resists wrinkling, works very well.

## Shadow-Puppet Stage Tools

➤ Carpenter's square: For use during construction of the screen frame, to make sure the frame is square while the glue dries.

➤ Saw: For cutting wood for the support frame.

➤ Drill: For drilling holes for bolts and pilot holes for screws, if necessary.

➤ Staple gun: For attaching hook-and-loop fasteners.

➤ Screwdriver: For the screws.

➤ Hammer: If you are using brads to attach the plywood.

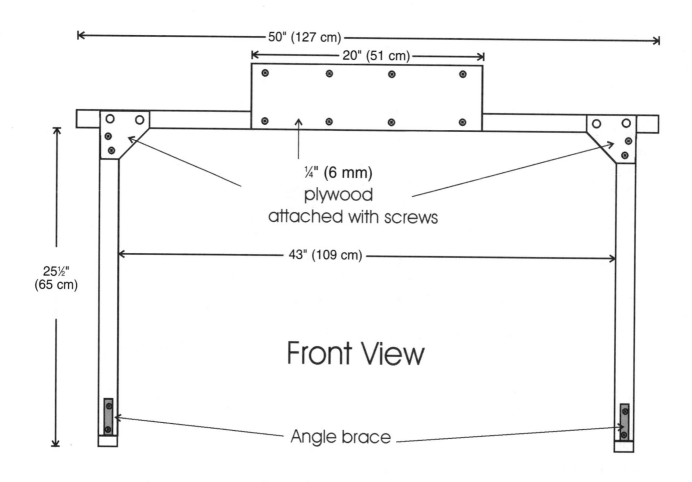

50" (127 cm)

20" (51 cm)

¼" (6 mm)
plywood
attached with screws

43" (109 cm)

25½"
(65 cm)

# Front View

Angle brace

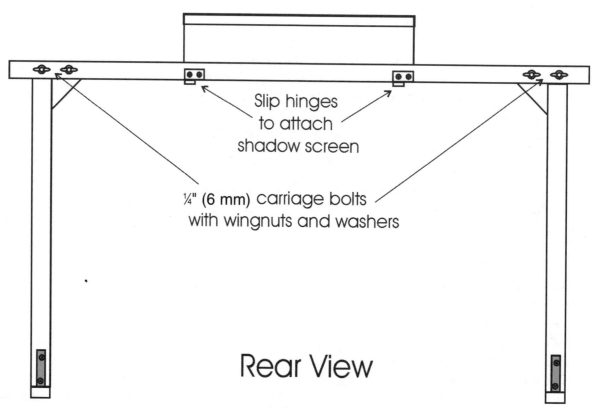

Slip hinges
to attach
shadow screen

¼" (6 mm) carriage bolts
with wingnuts and washers

# Rear View

*Shadow Screen Support Frame (Front and Rear Views)*

Puppets, Kids, and Christian Education © 2001 Augsburg Fortress. This page may be reproduced for local use.

The shadow-puppet stage consists of three parts: the shadow screen, the support frame, and the curtain. The shadow screen is assembled simply by applying glue to the grooves on the ends of each precut frame piece and putting the frame pieces together. Use a carpenter's square to make sure that the frame is square while the glue dries.

When the glue is dry, the shower curtain liner can be stretched over the screen. The liner should be cut big enough to cover the support frame and wrap around to the back. You should have enough liner on the back to reach just beyond the binder clips that will hold the liner in place. Attach the top edge of the liner to the frame with thumb tacks. The other edges are held to the frame with binder clips. Don't worry about creases in your shower curtain liner. After it has been stretched over the screen for a few days, they will disappear.

The shadow screen is the only "delicate" stage piece that you will need to store. The surface of the screen, the shower curtain liner, can easily be stretched beyond repair, if anything is leaned against it. We store our shadow screen in a large folder of corrugated cardboard that we constructed. The folder is closed with a couple of straps of hook-and-loop fasteners. Folding the wire loops of the

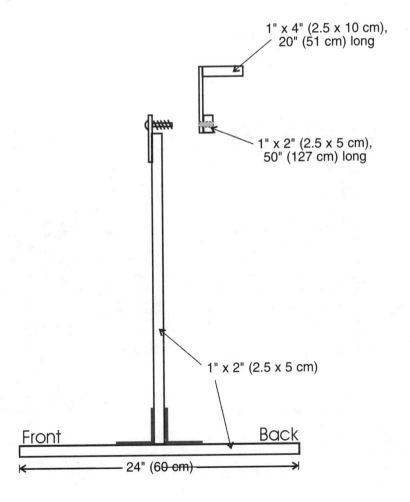

*Shadow Screen Support Frame (Side View)*

binder clips into the front of the screen can also stretch the surface, so we remove the wire loops from the binder clips on the front side of the screen before we store it. We keep these loops in a plastic zipper storage bag that we store with the screen.

The support frame for the shadow screen is constructed as shown in the diagrams on the previous pages. It is designed to be dismantled for easy storage. When dismantled, it will consist of three pieces: two side supports and a top crosspiece. The shadow screen is attached to the top crosspiece with the slip or loose pin hinges.

The curtain can be pleated or straight and is attached to the support frame with hook-and-loop fasteners.

## OBJECT THEATRE STAGE

We don't use a stage for object theatre. We use a table and a simple scrim backdrop on a frame. It consists of two upright supports and a crosspiece that supports the scrim backdrop. To keep the crosspiece on the upright supports, a finishing nail in the top of each upright support matches a hole in the crosspiece. The upright pieces are clamped to the table for support.

The simple scrim backdrop is a loose-weave black fabric. When you shine light on the front of the backdrop, you can't see through it from the front, but

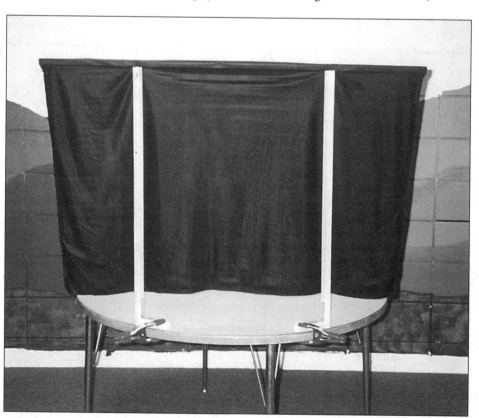

*Scrim Backdrop Frame*

the puppeteers behind it can see through to the lighted side. You will have to experiment in the fabric store to find the right fabric. Drape the fabric over your hand. Can you see your hand through the fabric? If so, the fabric is probably too thin. Hold it up to your face. Can you see through it easily? If so, it may work. Sometimes two fabrics used together will give you just the right effect.

The scrim fabric is sewn with a casing at the top that the wooden crosspiece slides into. The scrim should be just as long as the crosspiece, so there are no gathers in the fabric. The scrim should hang down to four or five inches above the tabletop.

## MULTIPURPOSE STAGE

The main stage that we use in our program was designed to work with several different types of puppetry. It can be used for handle-bag puppets or any other type of puppet operated from below, and it also works for marionettes operated from above.

Because handle-bag puppets are able to handle props well, we use a stage that includes a playboard. Playboard is the technical term in puppetry for a narrow shelf at the edge of the stage. Props can be set on the playboard and scenery can be attached to the playboard. The playboard should be at least 4" (10 cm) deep. Any narrower and your props are likely to fall off.

A scrim backdrop is another very useful feature on a puppet stage. It allows the puppeteers to stand behind the scrim backdrop and see their puppets as they perform. Theatrical scrim is a specific type of fabric that is only available through theatrical suppliers, but any of a variety of loose-weave fabrics can be used for a puppet stage backdrop. To keep the scrim hanging straight while the learners are reaching underneath it, add a hem at the bottom of the backdrop and insert a small metal chain. The chain should go the full width of the backdrop. Chain can be purchased at most hardware stores.

Our multipurpose stage consists of hinged wooden 1" x 2" (2.5 x 5 cm) frames. The panels fold flat for easy storage. There are two sections of panels. One of the sets of panels includes a proscenium, the opening in the stage where the puppets perform. If the stage is being used for puppets operated from below, the proscenium panels are on the top of the stage. For use with marionettes, the panels are switched.

Our stage panels were all made 36" (90 cm) tall, which we later realized was too short for puppets operated from below. We retro-fitted the solid set of panels with 12" (30 cm) long plywood legs to raise the playboard to a comfortable 48" (120 cm) off the ground.

## Multipurpose Stage Materials

➤ Lumber: (1" x 2"/2.5 x 5 cm pine) For the panel frames.

➤ Plywood: ( ½"/12 mm) For the playboard. Could also use 1" x 4" (2.5 x 10 cm) pine.

➤ Metal corner plates: For the support frame. Triangular corner plates made of ¼" (6 mm) plywood can also be used.

➤ Metal angle braces: For attaching the playboard to the stage panels.

➤ Hinges: (2"/5 cm) You'll need 12 of these to attach the frames together.

➤ Wood glue: For assembling the panels.

➤ Finishing nails: To keep the top set of panels from slipping off the bottom set.

➤ Hook-and-loop fasteners: (1"/2.5 cm wide) To attach curtain to stage.

➤ Fabric: For the stage curtain. Lightweight crushed velvet or robe velour, which has a velvet look to it but resists wrinkling, works well.

## Multipurpose Stage Tools

➤ Carpenter's square: To make sure the panels are square.

➤ Saw: For cutting wood for support frame.

➤ Drill: For drilling holes for bolts and pilot holes for screws, if necessary.

➤ Staple gun: For attaching the hook-and-loop fasteners.

➤ Screwdriver: For the screws.

Construct the stage as shown in the diagram on page 37.

Finishing nails in the bottom set of panels line up with holes in the top set of panels. The holes slip over the nails and keep the top set of panels from sliding off the bottom set of panels. There are two finishing nails in the top of each panel and two holes in the bottom of each panel.

The playboard is made of ½" (12 mm) plywood. It should be at least 4" (10 cm) deep and as long as the proscenium opening in your stage. It can also be made of 1" x 4" (2.5 x 10 cm) pine. The playboard has two angle braces and four short pieces of 1" x 2" (2.5 x 5 cm) attached to the bottom as shown below. The panel of the frame fits snugly between the angle braces and the blocks of 1" x 2" (2.5 x 5 cm) The panel is notched slightly to account for the thickness of the angle braces.

To support a scrim backdrop, you can construct a batten out of 1" x 2" (2.5 x 5 cm). Use a steel corner brace on each end of the board to attach the batten to the top side panels of the stage. A simple bolt latch can be used to secure the batten in place. Drill a hole in each of the two side panels large enough for the bolt to lock into.

## CURTAINS

The curtain on our stage has proven to be a much more important element in our puppetry program than we ever imagined. We created a pleated curtain of red crushed velvet, because we wanted the stage to look professional. We hoped that the professional look of our stage and puppets would set the tone for the program, and I think it has done that very well.

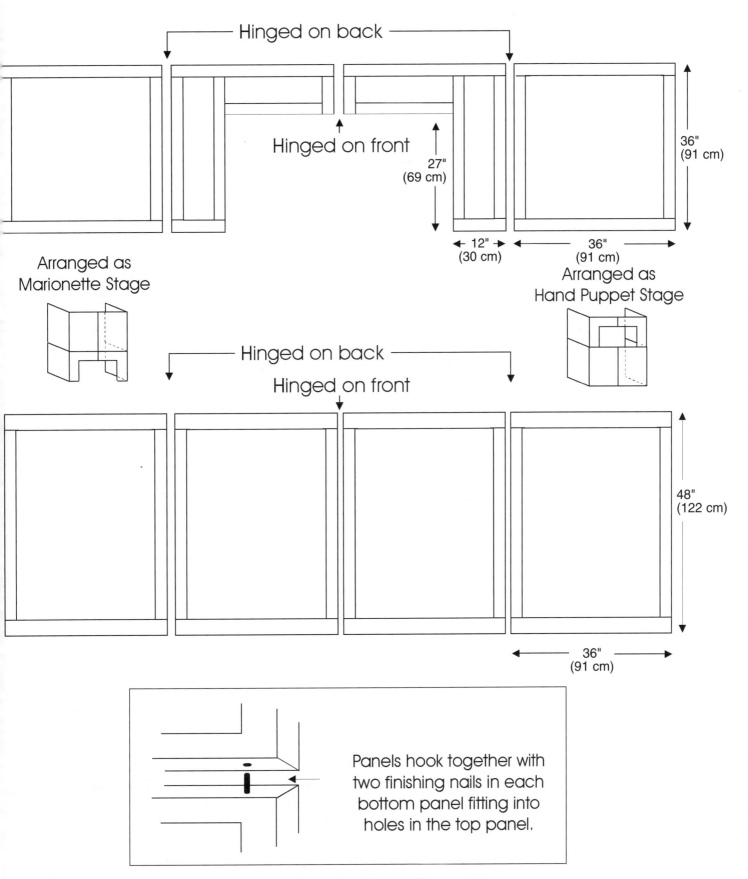

Hinged on back

Hinged on front

27" (69 cm)

36" (91 cm)

12" (30 cm)

36" (91 cm)

Arranged as Marionette Stage

Arranged as Hand Puppet Stage

Hinged on back

Hinged on front

48" (122 cm)

36" (91 cm)

Panels hook together with two finishing nails in each bottom panel fitting into holes in the top panel.

*Stage Construction and Finishing Nails*

What we didn't expect was how often the kids would notice, gravitate to, and comment on the curtain. The softness, color, and sheen of the curtain seem to attract them. The kids also seem to respond to the fact that a quality stage was put together just for them. They respect that and it translates into a respect for the work that we do with the puppets.

A lightweight fabric with a rich look, such as a crushed velvet, will work well for a curtain. Robe velour is another fabric that works well and comes in a variety of colors. For the multipurpose stage, you will need to make one curtain for each of the two sets of panels. The curtains will attach to the stage with 1" (2.5 cm) strips of hook-and-loop fasteners. On the stage, the hook-and-loop fasteners should be glued and stapled in place on the front and sides as close to the top edge as possible. We usually use the hook-and-loop fasteners on the wood and the loops on the fabric. This keeps the fabric from sticking to its own fasteners when we fold it for storage.

The curtain should be sewn so that when all the edges are hemmed, it is 1" (2.5 cm) taller than the panels that it will cover. Sew the hook-and-loop fasteners to the fabric 1" (2.5 cm) down from the top edge, so the curtain will extend slightly above the panels when it is attached. The curtain should also be wide enough to extend behind the stage a few inches on either side. Be sure to put a strip of hook-and-loop fasteners on the inside of the stage to catch the ends of either side of the curtain.

The curtain can either be constructed as a flat fabric covering for the panels or as a pleated covering. If you are using pleats (and it will look terrific with pleats), your fabric width will need to be two to three times the width of the panels.

## LIGHTING

With the exception of shadow puppetry, special lighting isn't required for your puppet performances. It does, however, add a great deal to the theatrical look of your performance and, consequently, to the excitement of the whole experience for your kids. We've found that "running the lights" is also a job that's very popular with the kids, even if it consists of nothing more than flipping a switch at the right time.

Simple clip lights, the kind that would usually be clipped to a shelf or a headboard, will do the job for you. You should be able to find clip lights that can handle a 40- or 60-watt bulb. Be sure not to exceed the wattage rating of the clip light you use.

A dimmer for your lights is also a useful tool. A very simple dimmer can be constructed with an extension cord and a lamp dimmer. The dimmer we used is described on its package as "lamp dimmer—lamp cord style." A cord-style dimmer is designed to be wired into the cord of a lamp to make an ordinary lamp dimmable. Normally, the cord of the lamp would be cut at the point where the dimmer switch was to be added and the dimmer would be wired in. You can do the same thing with an extension cord. Cut the extension cord where you want

the dimmer and follow the directions for wiring the dimmer into the cord. If you can't find a cord dimmer, you can use a standard wall dimmer switch and wire it into an electric box. Be sure to respect the wattage limit of the dimmer that you use and to only use it with incandescent lights. Our dimmer has a maximum rating of 150 watts.

Another option for lighting is to use overhead track lighting for your stage. It's a great convenience if you have the luxury of using existing track lighting or installing such lighting especially for use with your puppet stage. Track lighting makes it very easy to put the light where you need it, and you can generally use higher wattage bulbs than you can with clip lights. Having the dimmer or switch for the lights on the wall rather than behind the puppet stage also allows more room for puppeteers in the stage.

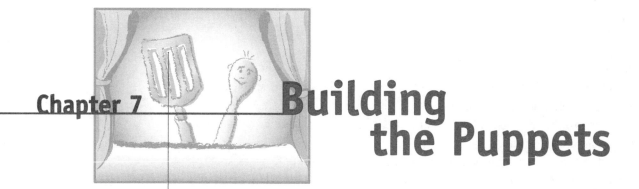

# Chapter 7

# Building the Puppets

You've probably noticed by now that there is no chapter on buying puppets. Unfortunately, the puppets that I believe work best for what we do aren't available commercially. The good news is that the puppets can all be constructed reasonably quickly and easily. My wife, Kathy, and I have conducted several hands-on puppet construction workshops and we've discovered that most people quickly get the knack of putting these puppets together.

Although the puppet construction is essentially a "no experience necessary" sort of operation, the crafters and sewers in your church will be the best people to turn to for some help. We've also had junior and senior high school students attend some of the puppet construction workshops and they've done very well. You might want to consider puppet construction as a youth group service project.

One approach is to "farm out" the construction work to various individuals, but we've found that getting a group together to work on the puppets in one place at one time also works well and can be a lot of fun.

*You might want to consider puppet construction as a youth group service project.*

## SHADOW PUPPETS

### Materials

➤ Black poster board: Most of the puppets will be cut from poster board.

➤ White tracing paper: For tracing the patterns onto the black poster board.

➤ Clear self-adhesive paper: Used with colored tissue paper to create shadows in color. Can also be used to reinforce the black poster board.

➤ Colored tissue paper: Used to make colored shadow puppets. Check craft stores for packs of tissue paper with multiple colors to a pack.

➤ Brass paper fasteners: (½"/12 mm long) For joints for moving parts.

➤ Welding rod or coat hanger wire: 1⁄16" (1 mm) diameter welding rod, available at welding supply stores, is straight and easy to work with, but coat hanger wire will also work.

➤ Clear tape: (½"/12 mm) Used to attach the wire rods to the colored shadow puppets. It may tear, so keep some on hand for quick repairs.

➤ Filament tape (½"/12 mm) Also called strapping tape, this reinforced tape is stronger and can be used on the opaque (black poster board) shadow puppets, where the filaments won't show up.

## Tools

➤ Scissors: To cut out puppets.

➤ Razor knife: To cut out small interior details.

➤ Cutting board: For use with the razor knife. A thick piece of corrugated cardboard will do.

➤ Stylus: To trace the pattern using the tracing paper. A dry pen also works.

➤ Wire cutter: To cut the welding rod or coat hanger wire.

➤ Needle-nose pliers: To bend the welding rod or coat hanger wire.

➤ Paper punch (optional): To make holes for the brass paper fasteners.

➤ Leather punch (optional): To make holes for the brass paper fasteners, if the paper punch won't reach deep enough.

➤ Hammer (optional): For use with the leather punch.

➤ Block of wood (optional): For use with the leather punch and hammer.

➤ Stapler: To staple the filament tape to the puppet.

## Basic Shadow Puppet Construction

The starting point for shadow puppet construction is the pattern. Most of the shadow puppets that we use are basically silhouettes. As you can see from the diagram on page 42, the designs are quite broad without lots of little details. I have designed most of our puppets myself, but I've taken the style of design from the late Roland Sylwester, a fine artist and puppeteer. His two books, "Teaching Bible Stories More Effectively With Puppets" and "The Puppet and the Word," give some of the best explanations and examples of puppetry in the church that I've seen. They are both, unfortunately, out of print, but check your local library.

You can also look to children's books for inspiration. When we did the story of creation, our Christian education director showed me a book about creation. The silhouettes of all the various animals caught in motion at the end of the book translated beautifully into shadow puppets.

Another idea source for shadow puppet designs are silhouette clip art books. Dover Publications, Inc., has produced a number of books of silhouettes that can be very helpful. Most major bookstores will carry a selection of this type of book. Several of the silhouette books are also available via mail order from the Puppeteers of America's Puppetry Store. Contact information for the Puppetry Store is available in the resources section at the end of this book.

Remember, the patterns for the shadow puppets don't have to be fancy. You're really better off if they aren't. The more complicated the design, the longer it will take to make the puppets. On top of that, small details may not show up well from a distance.

If you are making shadow puppets with moving parts, you will need to create a pattern for each piece and mark the pivot point where the hole for the paper fastener will be punched. Until you are comfortable designing shadow puppets with moving parts, it's a good idea to first make a simple paper mock-up puppet to make sure that you have the pivot point in the right place. See page 64 in the appendix for a shadow-puppet pattern.

# Moses and the Hebrew People

Moses

Pharaoh

*Moses Shadow Puppets*

Most of the shadow puppets will be made from black poster board covered with clear self-adhesive paper. The self-adhesive paper isn't absolutely necessary, but it will help the puppets hold up better. Once you have your patterns complete, you are ready to start construction.

Using your stylus (or dry pen), trace the pattern onto the poster board with the white tracing paper. The bottom layer is the poster board. The middle layer is the tracing paper, and the pattern is on top. It's helpful to tape one side of the pattern to the poster board, so you can lift up the pattern to make sure that you have traced it completely. Don't forget to trace the pivot point marks for the holes for any moving parts.

To reinforce the puppets so they will last longer, attach clear self-adhesive paper to both sides of the poster board. Do this after the pattern is traced, but before cutting the puppet out. The self-adhesive paper is only necessary if you want to use the puppets for several years.

Use your scissors and/or razor knife to cut out the pattern pieces.

Use the paper punch to punch out holes for any moving parts, where the pivot points were marked from the pattern. If the paper punch can't reach in far enough, you can use a leather punch or razor knife. The punch will give a much cleaner hole (and much smoother movement) than the razor knife, however. I put the shadow puppet on a wooden block and punch out the hole with a leather punch and a hammer.

Connect any moving parts with brass paper fasteners. The round heads of the paper fasteners should be on the side of the puppet that will be against the screen.

Cut a piece of welding rod or wire 12"-15" (30 to 40 cm) long. Bend one end of the wire into a hook as shown in the photo on page 44.

Attach the rod about two-thirds of the way up the puppet with the filament tape. The rod should be able to pivot easily. Staple filament tape to the puppet on either side of the wire. The smooth side of the staple should be on the "screen side" of the puppet. The rod for a moving arm (or other moving part with a wide range of movement) can be attached by bending a loop into the end of the rod and sewing the rod to the puppet. See photo on the following page.

You can also add a short piece of ¼" (6 mm) dowel to the end of each wire. The dowel will make the puppets easier to operate and will prevent anyone from being poked by the wire. This is a very common technique among professional puppeteers. We haven't found it necessary for the puppets that we've used in our program, however.

To add the dowel, drill a hole slightly smaller than the diameter of the wire into the end of the dowel and force the wire into the hole. You may need to use a little epoxy glue to keep the wire firmly in place.

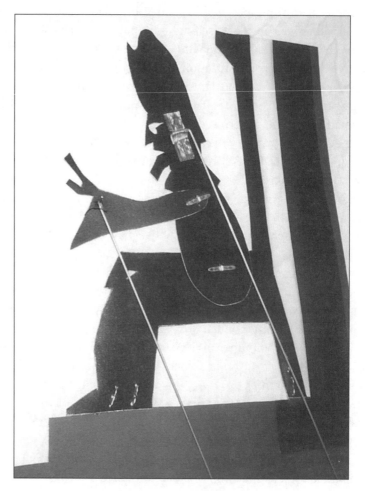

*Shadow Puppet with Rods Attached*

### Colored Shadow Puppet Construction

You can add color to opaque shadow puppets very easily. Cut the puppet out of black poster board as you would normally, but additionally cut out the interior area that you want to color. Cut a piece of colored tissue paper just bigger than the area that you cut out. On the front of the puppet, put a piece of clear self-adhesive paper over the area that you cut out. Turn the puppet over, so that the sticky side of the self-adhesive paper is facing up through the hole. Trim any bits of paper that reaches beyond the edges of the puppet.

You can now attach your tissue paper to the sticky side of the self-adhesive paper covering your cut-out area. The tissue paper should be at least ⅛" (3mm) from the outer edge of the puppet. Trim the tissue paper, if necessary. Cover your tissue paper with self-adhesive paper on this second side and cut off any that hangs over the edge.

You can also make shadow puppets that are all color, but the process is a little more difficult. When we did the story of Moses with shadow puppets, the burning bush was one of the best scenes. The bush was made of black poster

board, cut so that it was a loose mesh of branches and leaves. The fire was a separate puppet made of colored tissue paper and clear self-adhesive paper. The fire could be moved and seen as flames behind the bush.

The flames were cut individually from red, yellow, and orange tissue paper. The backing was peeled off of a piece of clear self-adhesive paper, which was then laid sticky side up. The various colored flames were each carefully positioned on the contact paper, since they couldn't be moved after they were put in place. After all the tissue paper pieces had been attached, a second piece of clear self-adhesive paper was added to cover the tissue from the other side, sealing the tissue paper between the two layers. Finally, the self-adhesive paper was trimmed up to the edge of the tissue paper.

For the colored shadow puppets, we attach the rods with clear tape rather than the filament tape. It is more prone to tearing, but it doesn't cast a shadow like the filament tape does.

## Additional Tricks

For our story of Moses, we needed to be able to represent the plague of flies, the plague of frogs, the plague of locust, etc. To do this, I drew one fly and three different frogs. We made multiple photocopies of these and pasted them together to make a page of flies and a page of frogs. (See diagram on page 46.) We photocopied these pages onto sheets of transparency and attached a wire rod to each sheet. With three sheets moving around, we could fill the shadow screen covering Moses and Pharaoh. We used the same three sheets for both the locust and the flies. As well as saving us a bit more puppet construction time, we were able to add a little humor to the script by mentioning that the plague of locusts "looked a lot like the flies."

For the story of creation, we started with a shadow screen devoid of any scenery. For the seas, we wrinkled up a large piece of blue tissue paper and sealed it between two sheets of clear self-adhesive paper. The top edge was cut with a simple wave pattern. It was cut to the length of the shadow screen, so that it could slide into place between the shadow screen and the frame. For the land, we used a large piece of corrugated cardboard. We cut it to the shape we wanted, about half the width of the shadow screen, and stapled strips of poster board to the bottom and side of it. The poster board was able to slide between the water and the frame of the shadow screen to hold it in place.

Along the top edge of our land, we attached a strip of hook-and-loop fasteners. On our trees and other plants, we attached strips of hook-and-loop fasteners. This way, the plants could grow up out of the land, get attached to the hook-and-loop fasteners on the land, and be left there as scenery.

Shadow puppetry lends itself to all sorts of interesting effects. As you try things out, you will probably discover other exciting things you can do.

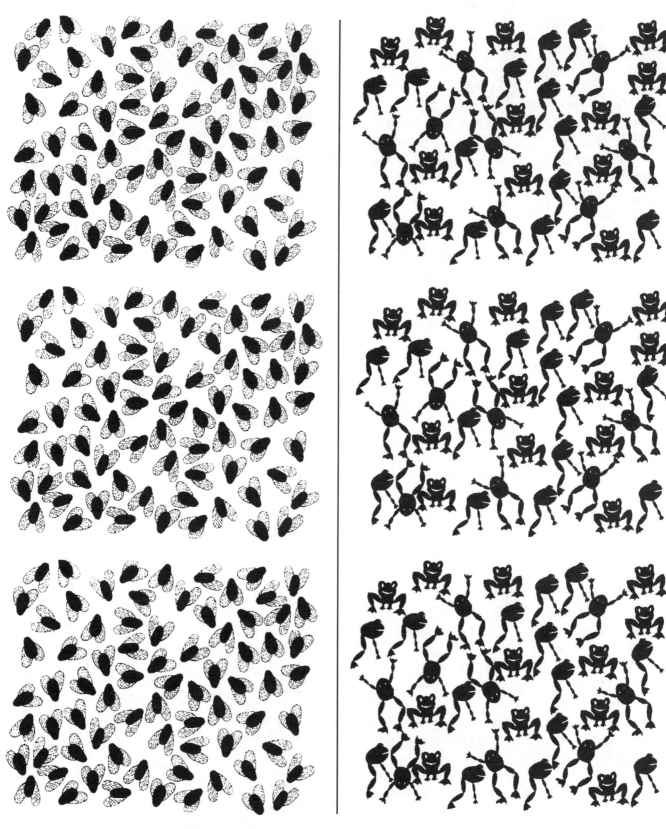

# Plagues of Flies and Frogs

## HANDLE-BAG PUPPETS

### Materials for the Head

*(The quantities and dimensions listed below are for one puppet.)*

➤ Dowel (¾" x 6¾"/0.75 x 17 cm): The handle for the head.

➤ Wood (1" x at least 2½" wide [2.5 x 6 cm]): I use pine, but anything you have handy will work just fine.

➤ Corrugated cardboard (two types—double thick and very thin): The double-thick cardboard looks like two pieces of corrugated cardboard glued together, which is essentially what it is. It is usually used in boxes for heavy items like computer monitors. The thin cardboard is not much thicker than the pressed cardboard used for the backs of note pads, but if you look closely, it has the wavy lines that are the mark of corrugated cardboard. You may find it used in boxes for shoes or bicycle helmets, for example. *Do not* use cardboard with a smooth shiny coating, because the glue will not be able to soak in and will not hold well.

➤ Wood glue: To glue the dowel into the wood.

➤ Felt: To cover the head and nose and also for the eyebrows. Stiffened felt works especially well for eyebrows.

➤ Fake fur: For hair, beards, and eyebrows.

➤ Fabric glue (solvent based): Also known as bridal adhesive, because it is used for making bridal veils.

*Pharoah Handle-Bag Puppet*

## Tools

➢ Saw: To cut the dowels to length and to cut out the wooden base. A band saw works very well and can also be used to cut out the double-thick corrugated cardboard. A coping saw will also do the job.

➢ Razor knife: To cut the double-thick corrugated cardboard.

➢ Cutting board: For use with the razor knife. A thick piece of corrugated cardboard will do.

➢ Drill or drill press: To drill the hole for the dowel. A drill press will give you a straight hole.

➢ ¾" (18 mm) drill bit: To use with the drill.

➢ Staple gun: To anchor the cardboard to the base.

➢ Scissors: To cut out the felt and thin cardboard

The basic handle-bag puppet consists of a head on a handle of some sort and a cloth bag that serves as the body. The head can be made of many different

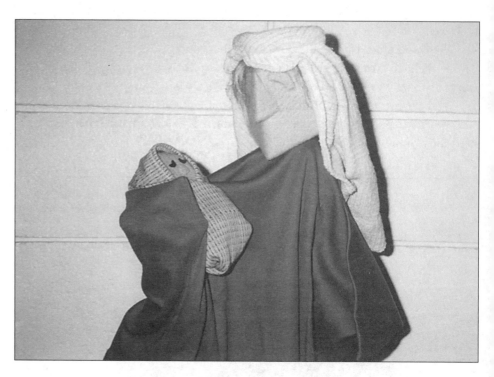

*Handle-Bag Puppet*

things. My design uses a wooden dowel placed in a wooden base with the head built up of double-thick corrugated cardboard. It's a quick method of construction that produces a good-looking result. The head could also be made of papier-mâché over foam, foam rubber, or a plastic bottle with a long, thin neck. The neck of the plastic bottle would become the handle for the puppet.

Our puppets were also designed with very simplified features. There were several reasons for this choice. I didn't want the puppets to have fixed expres-

sions—I wanted the mood of the puppet to come instead from the learner operating it. I also wanted to be able to reuse the puppets in a variety of different stories. The simplified features are more visible from farther away and also simplify the construction process a bit.

## Construction of the Head

### *Constructing the wooden center piece*

1. Trace the diamond wood pattern onto a piece of 1" (2.5 cm) wood. Make sure to mark the spot where the hole will be drilled. See page 65 in the appendix for the handle-bag puppet head wood pattern.

2. Drill a ¾" (18 mm) hole in the wood piece as marked.

3. Cut out the diamond piece with a band saw.

4. Cut a ¾" (18 mm) dowel to 6¾" (17 cm) long.

Glue the dowel into the hole in the diamond piece, so that one end of the dowel is flush with one end of the diamond.

### *Adding the cardboard to the head*

1. Trace the head pattern onto a piece of double-thick corrugated cardboard. See page 66 in the appendix for the handle-bag puppet head cardboard pattern. Mark the dotted line that ends at the chin. Corrugated cardboard has grain lines on the surface, and the chin should be pointing in the direction of the length of the grain. Also, the point of the chin should be centered between two grain lines.

2. Cut out the double-thick cardboard with a razor knife or band saw.

3. Fold the cardboard on the dotted line that ends at the chin. A ruler or straight piece of wood placed on the fold line as you fold will help you get a straight fold.

4. Hold the cardboard piece up against the wooden diamond piece to determine where the two side folds should be made. Make those folds.

5. Mark where one side meets the back of the diamond and cut the cardboard to length. Do the same with the other side, so the sides meet at the point of the diamond. This is the back of the head.

6. Glue the cardboard to the diamond with wood glue or white glue and staple it at the back. Don't staple it at the front, because the dents in the cardboard from the staples will show under the felt covering.

### *Covering the head with felt*

1. Cut a piece of felt 8½" x 12" (22 cm x 30 cm).

2. Starting with the back of the head, spread fabric glue very lightly over one of the two sections of the back of the head. Position the felt so that about ½" (12 mm) extends over onto the other back section, so that the felt will cover where the two ends of the cardboard come together. Glue this flap of felt down onto the other back section. Leave roughly 1½" (4 cm) of felt beyond the edge of the cardboard on the top and the bottom.

3. Repeat the gluing on each section, working your way around the head. Before gluing the last quarter on the back of the head, cut the felt so it will butt up against the other end of the felt without overlapping.

4. The felt extending beyond the cardboard on the top and bottom will be folded and glued to the inside of the head. Cut notches in the felt at the folds in the cardboard, so the felt won't bunch up when it is glued down.

### *Finishing the Head—Noses, Eyebrows, and Hair*

1. Select or design a nose pattern and trace the nose onto very thin corrugated cardboard. See page 67 in the appendix for sample nose and eyebrow patterns.

2. Cut the nose out of the cardboard.

3. Fold the nose as indicated on the pattern.

4. With the nose folded into its final shape, glue felt to the nose with fabric glue. It is important to glue the felt on after the cardboard is folded. If the nose is flat, when the felt is glued on, the felt will keep the nose from folding.

5. Glue the nose to the head with fabric glue. You will need to hold the nose in position for a couple of minutes until the glue dries. Make sure not to put the nose too high on the head. There should be plenty of room for eyebrows and a headpiece above the nose.

6. Select or design an eyebrow pattern and trace the eyebrows onto felt, stiffened felt, or fake fur.

7. Cut the eyebrows from the felt.

8. Position the eyebrows on the head. Make sure you know just where you want them before gluing. The position and angle of the eyebrows will set the character of the puppet.

9. Glue the eyebrows to the head one at a time.

10. Add hair to the puppet, beard, mustache, and other details if desired.

## Materials for Bag and Headpiece

(*The quantities and dimensions listed below are for one puppet.*)

➤ Fabric glue (solvent based): Also known as bridal adhesive, because it is used for making bridal veils.

➤ Fabric for body: (45"/113 cm wide x 15"/38 cm tall) Select solid fabrics or those with very small patterns. A large pattern would be out of scale on a small puppet. Also look for fabrics that don't wrinkle, such as heavier knits or interlock or heavy woven fabrics like wool. Especially avoid stiff fabrics.

➤ Fabric for headpiece: (21"/58 cm wide x 14"/33 cm long) Select light-colored fabrics that are either solid or have a small print. Almost any lighter weight fabric will do.

➤ Fabric for Pharaoh's headpiece: (19"/48 cm x 14"/33 cm) Select fabrics that are shiny or glitzy with a small print.

➤ Corrugated cardboard: For Pharaoh's headpiece.

➤ Elastic: (¼"/6 mm) For headpieces.

## Tools

➤ Scissors: To cut out felt and thin cardboard.

➤ Sewing machine and/or serger: For sewing the fabric body.

## Construction of Bags

1. Fold the 45" (113 cm) length of the fabric in half to make a 15" x 22½" (38 x 56 cm) piece. Sew a seam with a ¼" (6 mm) seam allowance up the 15" (38 cm) end of the fabric to make a tube. Mark the center at the fold with a pin.

2. Line the seam up with your center pin mark.

3. Mark ⅝" (1.5 cm) on either side of your center pin mark. This will be the hole for the rod to fit through. Stitch from this mark to the outside edge with a ¼" (6 mm) seam allowance. Stitch the other side of the outside edge to finish off the top. Be sure not to close your center hole. If stitching with a sewing machine, reinforce the seams with a zigzag stitch.

4. Turn the bag right side out.

5. At the center hole, fold down each side ¼" (6 mm) and stitch this down the length of the hole on either side. This will finish off the hole opening for the puppet handle.

## Construction of Head Pieces for Handle-Bag Puppets

See pages 68-69 in the appendix for women's and men's sample headpiece patterns.

1. Cut a piece of fabric 21" (53 cm) wide x 14" (35 cm) long.

2. Zigzag or serge the four edges of the fabric.

3. Turn under one 21" (53 cm) edge of fabric ¼" (6 mm) and stitch down with a straight stitch. This will be the edge closest to the face of the puppet when finished.

4. On the wrong side of the fabric trace your pattern for the elastic with a pencil. To do so, find the center front of the fabric by folding the 21" (53 cm) width of the fabric in half. Mark the center front with a pin. Draw the pattern onto the wrong side of the fabric with a pencil, marking the center front and back and special lines at the front of the headpiece for the elastic placement. Be sure to match up the pattern to the fold line on your fabric.

5. With an 11" (28 cm) length of ¼" (6 mm) elastic, overlap the ends by ¼" (6 mm) and use a zigzag stitch to sew the ends together, making a circle of elastic.

6. Fold your circle of elastic together with the seam at one end. Mark the other end with a pin.

7. Pin the seam on your elastic circle to the center back marking on your fabric. The opposite point on your circle, marked with the pin, is pinned to the center front marking on your fabric.

8. For the elastic placement at the front of each headpiece, measure the elastic to the length needed, 3¼" (9 cm) for men and 1½" (4 cm) for women. Make sure it is an even amount on either side of the center front mark. The two lengths are different because the front of the women's headpiece is gathered

more than the men's. Pin the elastic to the fabric at the special markings penciled on the fabric from the pattern. The women's headpiece has a second special marking on either side of the center front. Measure 1" (2.5 cm) of elastic on each side and pin to the special marking.

9. Pin the rest of the elastic to the fabric evenly around the circle.

10. Using a zigzag stitch, stretch the elastic as you stitch it to the fabric around your circle. It is important to stretch the elastic along the pencil mark as you stitch or the headpiece will not fit the puppet well.

## Construction of Pharaoh's Headpiece

See page 70 in the appendix for a sample Pharaoh's headpiece pattern.

1. The headpiece will be made from a piece of fabric 19" (48 cm) wide x 14" (35 cm) tall. You will need a piece of ¼" (6 mm) elastic that is 4" (10 cm) long.

2. Zigzag or serge the four edges of the fabric.

3. Cut the stiffener for the front of the headpiece out of cardboard. Fold the stiffener on the fold line. Mark the tabs on the cardboard with a pencil.

4. Cut the ¼" (6 mm) elastic to length (one piece, 4"/10 cm long). At the tab mark on the cardboard, overlap ½" (12 mm) of elastic and attach it to the cardboard with six or eight zigzag stitches. Make sure not to puncture the cardboard too many times with the needle, because that may cause the elastic to rip out. Repeat on the other side to form a circle with the stiffener and the elastic. Glue around the edges of the elastic and the cardboard to add strength using fabric glue.

5. Fold the 19" (48 cm) length of fabric in half and use a pin to mark the center front. Match the center front of the fabric with the fold of the cardboard. Glue the edge of the 19" (48 cm) length of the fabric to the straight edge of the cardboard stiffener with fabric glue. The side of the cardboard stiffener that the elastic was sewn to will be the inside of the headpiece. The fabric is glued to the outside of the headpiece.

6. Using the pattern as a guide, fold the fabric under on the fold line bringing line 1 down to line 2 to form a pleat. Glue in place.

## Beards

➤ Beards can be made of fake fur, felt, or yarn.

➤ Use buckram (drapery-pleat stiffener) as a backing for beards.

➤ The beards can be attached with elastic for versatility.

## CROWD PUPPET

A variation on the handle-bag puppet that has been very useful for us is a multiheaded puppet that we've used to represent all of Joseph's brothers, an army, and various groups of servants and family.

*Crowd Puppet*

When we were putting together the story of Joseph, of multicolored coat fame, we needed to be able to represent all of his brothers, because they are so important to the action of the story. However we portrayed the brothers, they needed to be able to act and react. They had to be able to react when Joseph told them his dreams, and they needed to be able to gang up on Joseph. Using a puppet for each brother was impractical. We didn't have room for that many puppeteers behind our stage.

Our solution was to create a new type of handle-bag puppet that was no handle and all bag. Instead of the puppeteer placing one hand in a corner of the bag to be the puppet's hand, the puppeteer puts one hand in each of the two corners of the bag. Between the puppeteer's two hands in the bag is a sheet of 1" (2.5 cm) thick foam rubber, which supports the multiple heads.

## Materials

➤ Foam core (¼"/6 mm thick): The base for the heads. Thick corrugated cardboard can be substituted for the foam core.

➤ Felt: To cover the heads and for the features and hair.

➤ Foam rubber (1"/2.5 cm thick): Support in the body of the puppet.

➤ Spray adhesive (optional): Can be used to help hold the foam in the body.

➤ Fabric glue (solvent based): Also known as bridal adhesive, because it is used for making bridal veils.

➤ Fabric: A woven medium-weight fabric with a colorful geometric design of various stripes and a black, knit, medium-weight fabric such as robe velour. Strips of various fabrics, varying in width 2" to 4" (3 to 10 cm) or so, can be sewn together and used in place of the colorful fabric, as shown in the photograph above. The puppet in the photograph also uses black fabric behind the heads, which is not necessary and not described in these instructions.

## Tools

➤ Razor knife or band saw: To cut the foam core.

➤ Cutting board: For use with the razor knife. A thick piece of corrugated cardboard will do.

➤ Scissors: To cut the foam rubber and felt.

➤ Sewing machine or serger: To sew the bag for the body.

## Construction of the Heads

See pages 71-72 in the appendix for sample crowd puppet head patterns and layout.

1. Trace the head patterns onto the foam core.

2. Using the razor knife or band saw, cut out the heads.

3. Cut a piece of felt for each head. The felt pieces should be at least half an inch longer and wider than the head that is being covered. Select a few different colors of felt and decide how you want the flesh tones arranged in the crowd.

4. On each head, glue the felt to the surface of the foam core head with fabric glue. At each corner of the head, cut a notch in the felt. Glue the felt down over the edges of the head. The heads on the top row also have felt on the back, because they extend up past the top of the bag.

5. Trim the extra felt or glue it to the back of the head.

6. Cut hair, noses, and beards for the heads. Keep in mind how you will have the heads arranged on the crowd body.

## Construction of the Body

When stitching, use a (¼"/6 mm) seam allowance. You can either serge the seams or stitch with a straight stitch on a sewing machine. If you use a straight stitch, reinforce each seam with a zigzag stitch.

1. Cut the colorful fabric into a piece that is 28½" (71 cm) wide x 45" (113 cm) tall.

2. Fold the fabric in half with right sides together so that the fabric 28½" (71 cm) wide x 22½" (56 cm) tall. (The right side of the fabric will be the outside of the puppet body.) The folded edge is the top of the puppet.

3. Measure down from the folded edge 5" (13 cm) and in from each side 6¼" (16 cm). Draw a line for each of these measurements. This marks a rectangle at the top of each side of the puppet.

4. Following the lines you have drawn, stitch from the top of the folded edge down and follow the line out to the side. Repeat for the other side.

5. Sew the side seams together, beginning at the stitching line you just completed down to the bottom of the puppet.

6. At the top of the puppet on each side, you have a rectangle area marked with the stitching. Leaving a (¼"/6 mm) seam allowance, cut out the rectangle of fabric.

7. Cut through the seam allowance in each corner, right up to the seam but being careful not to cut into the stitching. This will help ease the corner when you turn the fabric right side out.

8. Turn your fabric right side out and pull the corners out to make right angles.

9. Serge or zigzag around the bottom edge of the colorful fabric. Turn ¼" (6 mm) of fabric to the inside of the puppet and straight stitch around to form a hem.

10. On the right side or outside of the colorful fabric, sew a straight stitch from the bottom of the puppet to the top, 6" (15 cm) in from each side seam.

### Finishing the Crowd

1. Cut a piece of 1" (2.5 cm) thick foam rubber into a piece 13" (33 cm) wide x 15½" (39 cm) tall.

2. Apply spray adhesive to one side of the foam.

3. Insert the foam into the middle pocket in the body with the adhesive side toward the back of the puppet body.

4. Arrange the heads on the body. Allow as much space between heads as you can.

5. Using fabric glue, attach each head to the body. Remember that the heads for the top row extend above the body, so they have felt on the back as well as the front.

## SPECIALTY PUPPETS

In addition to the crowd puppet, we have built a few other puppets, such as a baby, flock of sheep, Goliath, and a glowing angel, to fill special needs.

The baby we use is actually more of a prop than a puppet, since it isn't built to move on its own. It's only held by other puppets. We built our baby out of a 2" (5 cm) thick piece of foam rubber about 2½" (6 cm) wide x 5 (13 cm) long. To cut the foam we used an electric carving knife. You can also use a scissors to cut the foam, but the carving knife is much easier. We cut off all of the corners until

our block of foam was more potato shaped. We cut a large oval of felt for the face and glued it on with fabric glue, then wrapped a piece of fabric around the baby like a blanket. Once it was wrapped as we wanted, and we were sure all edges of the felt oval (the face) were covered, we glued the fabric in place. Finally, we drew on the facial features with a fine-tipped permanent marker.

On the first baby we made, our mistake was making it too big. What was comfortable in an adult hand was too big to be easily held by a child. Remember that all the hand props need to be small enough for the hands of the smallest children who will be using them.

Our flock of sheep is one of my favorite puppets. The whole flock is supported by one rod, and only one sheep is directly attached to that rod. The other sheep are all suspended from the rod or from the other sheep with elastic.

The sheep are cut from foam core. The feet and faces are painted black with short-nap fake fur glued on the bodies. The support is a "T" of ¼" (6 mm) x ¾" (18 mm) screen-door molding. The "T" is built into the top front sheep, which is viewed from both sides. All other sheep are only seen from one side. The other top sheep are suspended from the "T" with ½" (12 mm) black elastic. The bottom sheep are hung from the feet of the top sheep.

When we presented the story of David and Goliath, we used an idea that we learned from someone attending one of our workshops. For a vacation Bible school project, he built puppets on cardboard fabric bolts. Fabric stores will give them to you for no charge, and the bolts are lightweight and sturdy.

For Goliath, I cut slots in a cardboard fabric bolt near the bottom, so I could fold the slots in, glue them down, and form a handle. We glued felt to the top of the bolt for the face and added eyebrows, nose, and hair as we would for any handle-bag puppet. The body was a simple fabric bag glued to the body. One corner of the bag (Goliath's left hand) was folded in and attached to the body. The other corner was attached to a dowel that we had outfitted with a foam spearhead. The spear was used to operate Goliath's right hand.

## SPECIAL EFFECTS

For each new story that we do, I like to try out new ways of doing things. For the story of Jacob and Esau, I decided to use black light for the angels. I mounted a small fluorescent black light fixture above the puppets at the top of the proscenium of the puppet stage. (The proscenium is the opening in the stage where the puppets perform.) The angels and ladder in Jacob's dream were simple stick puppets made out of fluorescent poster board and glued to screen-door molding. For the angel that Jacob wrestles, I used a standard handle-bag puppet, but the head and costume bag were made of white fabric that glowed under fluorescent light. For the scenes with the angels, we dimmed the lights a little bit and turned on the fluorescent black light.

Black light is a wonderful effect, especially if used sparingly for special emphasis. The most difficult thing about black light effects, however, is that you can't tell what fabrics and other materials will glow under black light without

*For each new story that we do, I like to try out new ways of doing things.*

actually testing them. Some people will actually take a black light fixture with them to the fabric store, find an outlet, and start checking out fabrics. There are also small battery-powered, hand-held fluorescent black lights, which can make the shopping much easier. They are hard to find, but you may be able to find them online. Check www.collegesuppliers.com, www.hollywoodlights.com, or other sites you may find.

## ASSORTED PROPS

Props will help set the scene, give the puppets more options for "doing things," and can help emphasize important points in a story. Items like cups and bowls can frequently be found at garage sales or secondhand stores. Keep in mind that hand-held props need to be small enough for the smallest hands to grasp them easily. Items like altars and puppet-sized tents, though, will need to be made. You can really use your church's crafters and sewers to help you design and build props to enhance your stories.

Our stone altar was carved from foam and covered with papier-mâché. Because thick foam is fairly expensive, we actually used the expanding foam insulation that comes in a can. We sprayed mounds of foam onto cardboard to make the rocks for our altar.

Papier-mâché is a great way to make strong props that will last. Red rosin roofing paper makes very strong papier-mâché. Use two parts yellow carpenters' glue to one part water for the glue. To finish the alter we painted it with Deco Art brand Sandstones™ acrylic paint. This paint actually gives you a sandstone look just by brushing it on.

Our tent is just a fabric tube covering and suspended between two dowels. The wooden bases for the dowels can be fashioned with clothespins to clamp to the playboard on the stage.

We've sometimes used signs to make a point in a particular story. For the story of Abraham and Sarah, we made signs that said "Ha Ha Ha," "Ho Ho," and "Hee Hee." We used these laughing signs to punctuate Sarah's laughter, when she was told that she would have a son. We wanted to emphasize that the name of their son, Isaiah, means laughter. Signs can be made from poster board or foam core. Screen-door molding, ¼" x ¼" (6 x 18 mm), makes good handles.

## OBJECT THEATRE PUPPETS

Remember how I said there wasn't a section on buying puppets? Well, this section is as close as we're going to get. All of the items that we use for object theatre are either purchased at secondhand stores, garage sales, or surplus stores, or they are recovered from garages, attics, and other places around people's homes.

There is actually a bit of an art to finding good objects. I've tried to select a variety of colors, shapes, and sizes of objects, so they can be used to represent people, buildings, or other things. It's also helpful to have a majority of objects

that can stand on their own to represent people. This way a puppeteer can operate an object when it needs to be doing something, and then leave it standing as a quiet observer while the puppeteer goes on to operate some other object for a moment.

Old towels or bits of fabric are useful for turning into rivers, curtains, grass, and so on. When we did the story of Saul's conversion, one group of kids made a special point of using a blue towel as a river, so that Saul could slide under the towel for baptism by immersion.

Another thing to keep in mind, when hunting for performing objects, is to avoid objects that will be particularly interesting on their own. If a kid would rather play with one of the objects than be involved in the story, you probably need to pull that object out of the line-up. Consequently, items like balls or other toys aren't a good choice.

## CONCLUSION

Working together to create and perform a puppet show can bring a great sense of cooperation and community to a group of learners in a Sunday school. Similarly, working together to create a puppetry program for your Sunday school can strengthen community among adults, youth, and children. Don't try to do it all by yourself. The ideas, the work, and the final product will all be stronger if it's done as a group effort. Best of all, it will be fun—a fun way to involve new people into your Sunday school program and a fun way for the children of your church to learn and develop an appreciation for the important stories of our faith.

# Resources for Puppet Ministry

# Chapter 8

## ORGANIZATIONS

**The Fellowship of Christian Puppeteers**
107 Moore Allen St.
Dudley, NC 28333
www.fcpfellowship.org

The national organization for Christian puppeteers, ventriloquists, and clowns publishes a quarterly newsletter and hosts yearly festivals.

**The Puppeteers of America**
Membership Office
P.O. Box 29417
Parma, OH 44129-0417
(888) 568-6235
E-mail: PofAjoin@aol.com
www.puppeteers.org

The national organization for puppeteers in the United States offers an excellent quarterly publication, The Puppetry Journal, and sponsors national and regional puppetry festivals on alternating years. Members can make use of a video lending library with several hundred selections featuring all forms of puppetry performances as well as workshops. Consultants are also available to answer member queries on topics ranging from humor to religion to sound and lighting.

**UNIMA-USA**
1404 Spring St. N.W.
Atlanta, GA 30309-2820
(404) 873-3089
E-mail: unima@mindspring.com
www.unima-usa.org

UNIMA-USA is the American Chapter of Union Internationale del la Marionette, the world's oldest theatre organization. The organization's mission is to promote international understanding and friendship through the art of puppetry. UNIMA-USA fulfills its mission in a range of formal and informal ways,

but especially by encouraging and providing contacts to North American puppeteers traveling throughout the world and providing the same courtesy to international puppeteers traveling in North America.

## INTERNET RESOURCES

### Mailing Lists

Explore these mailing lists or search for others on your own.

#### christpup

An active e-mail mailing list that averages 10 messages a day. Most subscribers are active with puppet teams using moving-mouth hand puppets. There's usually more exchange of general fellowship and support than of information. To subscribe, send an e-mail message to: maillist@oac.u-net.com with the request "SIGNON christpup" in the subject field.

#### pupcrit

Although less active than christpup, the subscribers to this list have experience with a wide range of puppetry forms. This is a good list for technical information. To subscribe, send an e-mail to: majordomo@lists.village.virginia.edu with the request "SUBSCRIBE pupcrit" in the body of the message.

### Web Sites

**The Puppetry**
www.sagecraft.com

The most amazing puppetry spot on the Web. You can get anywhere from here.

**The Hunter Marionettes**
www.HunterMarionettes.com

The author's Web page with information and resources on puppet ministry, marionettes, and performances.

## BOOKS, PUPPETS, PATTERNS, AND MORE

**The Puppetry Store**
Auburn, Washington
(253) 883-8377
www.puppeteers.org

This service of the Puppeteers of America is the most complete resource available for puppetry books, patterns, scripts, and videotapes. The directors are also active Christian puppeteers with a wealth of personal experience.

**One Way Street, Inc.**
Englewood, Colorado
(303) 790-1188
(800) 569-4537
www.onewaystreet.com

One of the leading resources for Christian puppetry, they sell a variety of moving-mouth hand and rod puppets as well as scripts, stages, lighting and sound equipment, and a variety of other resources. They also present workshops across the country.

**Puppet Productions**
DeSoto, Texas
(972) 709-7400
(800) 854-2151
www.puppetproductions.com

Another of the leading resources for Christian puppetry, they also sell a variety of moving-mouth hand and rod puppets as well as scripts, stages, etc.

# Appendix Patterns

*All patterns included here are actual size. Do not enlarge them.*

# PARABLE PRODUCTIONS

presents

# Joshua at the Walls of Jericho

**starring**

*Sample Credits Sheet*

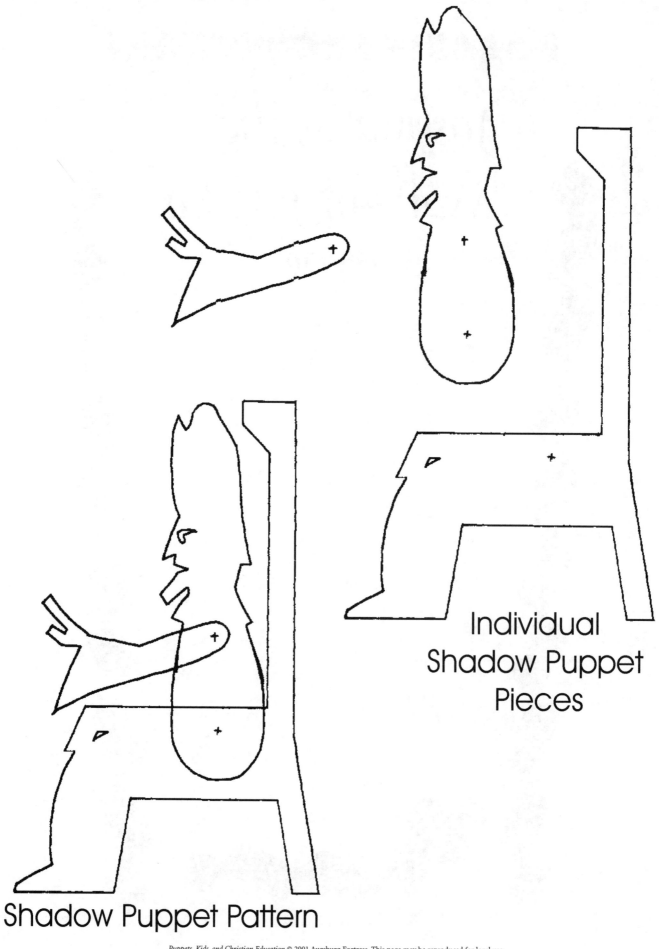

Individual
Shadow Puppet
Pieces

Shadow Puppet Pattern

## Patterns are actual size.
## Do not reduce.

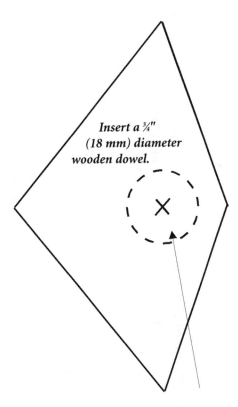

*Insert a ¾"*
*(18 mm) diameter*
*wooden dowel.*

**Hole for a ¾" (18 mm) diameter dowel.**
**Dowel should be 6¾" long.**

*Handle-Bag Puppet*
*Head Diamond Wood Pattern*

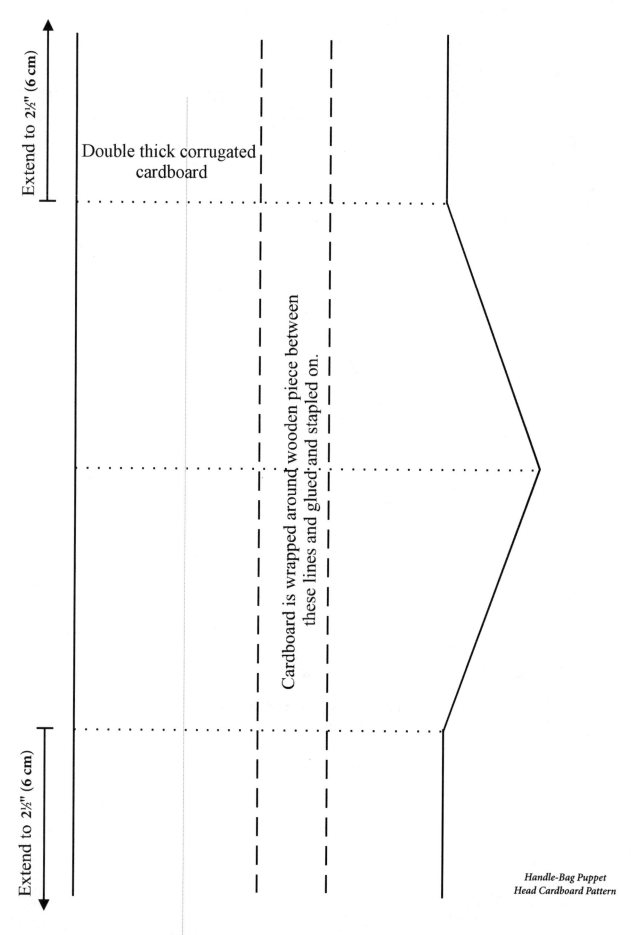

Extend to 2½" (6 cm)

Double thick corrugated cardboard

Cardboard is wrapped around wooden piece between these lines and glued and stapled on.

Extend to 2½" (6 cm)

*Handle-Bag Puppet*
*Head Cardboard Pattern*

# Sample Nose Patterns

## Normal Flat Nose

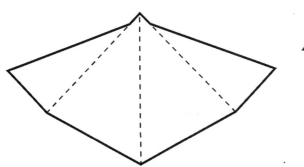

## Sharp Pointed Nose

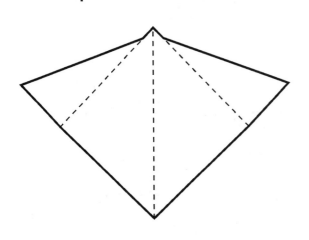

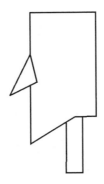

## Long Broad Nose

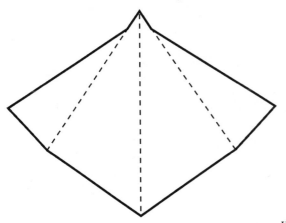

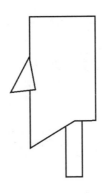

## Sample Eyebrow Patterns

### Harsh (Evil)

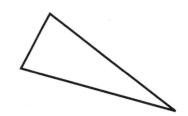

### Neutral

### Friendly

*Handle-Bag Puppet*
*Nose and Eyebrow Patterns*

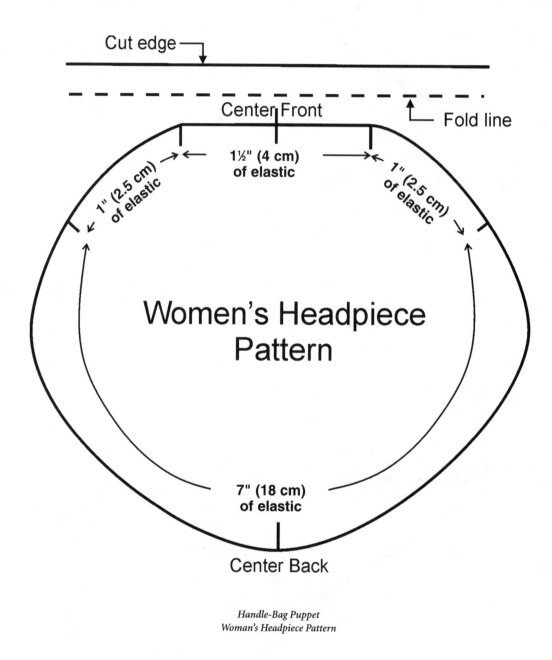

## Patterns are actual size.
## Do not reduce.

Cut edge ⎯

Center Front

Fold line

1" (2.5 cm) of elastic

1½" (4 cm) of elastic

1" (2.5 cm) of elastic

# Women's Headpiece Pattern

7" (18 cm) of elastic

Center Back

*Handle-Bag Puppet*
*Woman's Headpiece Pattern*

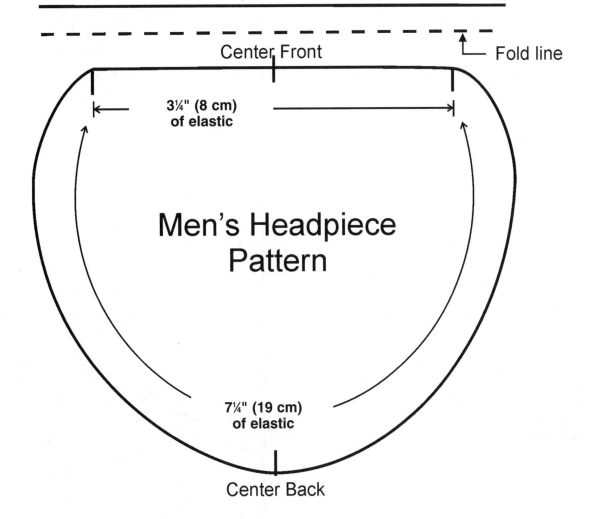

Cut edge

Center Front

Fold line

3¼" (8 cm)
of elastic

Men's Headpiece
Pattern

7¼" (19 cm)
of elastic

Center Back

*Handle-Bag Puppet*
*Men's Headpiece Pattern*

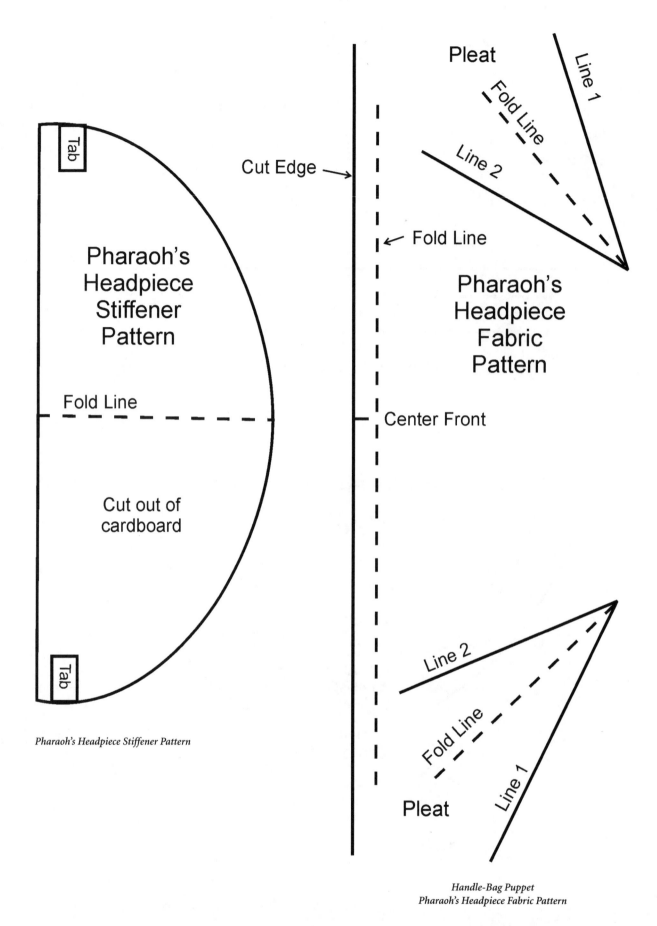

Pleat

Line 1

Fold Line

Line 2

Cut Edge →

Fold Line

Pharaoh's
Headpiece
Stiffener
Pattern

Pharaoh's
Headpiece
Fabric
Pattern

Tab

Tab

Fold Line

Center Front

Cut out of
cardboard

Line 2

Fold Line

Line 1

Pleat

*Pharaoh's Headpiece Stiffener Pattern*

*Handle-Bag Puppet*
*Pharaoh's Headpiece Fabric Pattern*

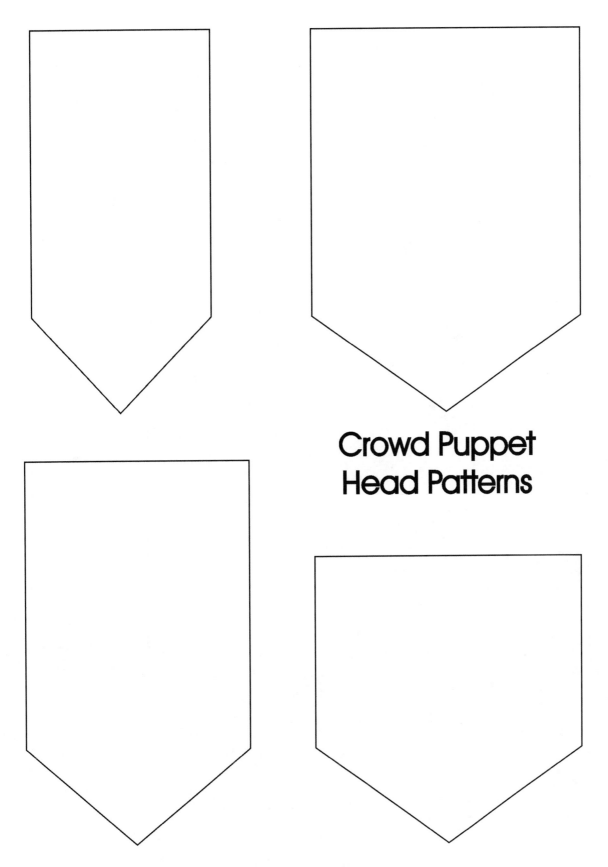

# Crowd Puppet
# Head Patterns

*Handle-Bag Puppet*
*Crowd Puppet Head Patterns*

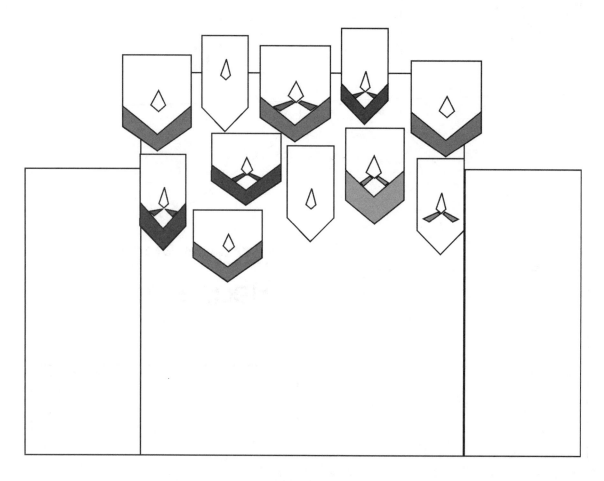

*Handle-Bag Puppet*
*Crowd Puppet Sample Layout*